PROCEED
WITHOUT
DELAY

BY THE SAME AUTHOR

% Postmaster

Proceed Without Delay

Thomas R. St. George

Thomas Y. Crowell Company
New York

TO MY

"Dear Folks"

INTRODUCTION

THE LAST TIME I SAW OZZIE ST. GEORGE was in the office of *Yank*, the Army enlisted men's magazine, in Sydney, Australia, late in May 1944. He was leaning back in a chair, and his feet were propped up on a desk. He had just come back from several months in back-country New Guinea and adjacent areas—places that in peacetime no white man would think of visiting unless he was (1) looking for gold; (2) raising coconuts; (3) a government officer handling native affairs; (4) a missionary; (5) a very intrepid traveler; or (6) crazy.

But Ozzie, in common with several thousand other Americans and a lot of Australians, had gone in, had lived through it, and now had returned to the mainland, as he says, to "have his malaria." His thin face was somewhat thinner than usual, and he had an atabrine "tan" —a nice name for a shade that is really a sickly dirty yellow—but so did I, after having spent five months in those precincts myself.

So there was no envy lost on Ozzie for that, but I couldn't help but admire one thing; he had acquired, somewhere "up north," a resplendent pair of Air Corps flying boots—a sort of oversized cowboy boot with a lot of wool fuzz sticking out the tops. They are all right at 10,000 feet in the air, but in Sydney—

"So they *do* look out of place," said Ozzie in answer to my unuttered comment. "Well, if you got something like these gorgeous things for free, what would you do?"

I guess there was no answer to that.

Also I couldn't help but admire, and still do, Ozzie's knack for putting the "little things" that go on about him into words so vividly and typically G.I., and so accurately descriptive, that it pays to read well what he writes. He does it with an ability that many an older and more "experienced" writer can well envy.

From such material the people of tomorrow will form their impressions of what our men are going through today. More power to him.

LEWIS B. SEBRING, JR.

New York City

[Mr. Sebring is a good friend of Ozzie St. George's for he spent twenty-seven months with Ozzie as a New York *Herald Tribune* war correspondent in the Southwest Pacific.]

PREFACE

(SYDNEY, AUSTRALIA)—Having but recently had my frame climbed by a number of the otherwise friendly natives for saying some things that, so they claim, must certainly lead the other peoples of the world to think of dear old Aussie as a land of gin and sin, I'm taking no chances this time. *Proceed Without Delay* will, I hope, amuse you. It may, perhaps, add something to your grasp of this Pacific War. Beyond that its aims disappear in the blue murk of the Owen Stanleys.

Thanks to *Yank* Magazine and a thick sheaf of travel orders published by Hq USASOS, APO 501, I've had, since July 1943, the rather unique opportunity of seeing a great deal of this much discussed theater, the Southwest Pacific. From one end to the other, from Sydney to Cape Gloucester, from the very best to the very worst. What I saw, what I did, what happened to me—those are the things I've written about. Where views are expressed, they are those generally held by very ordinary GIs, and they may or may not, therefore, in some instances, necessarily agree with the views of the Office of War Information, the Australian Department of Information, press relations officers anywhere, or the Committee of Five Senators.

Some of the things I saw (and some of the things I did, even, since July 1943) will probably shock hell out of sundry mothers, wives and sweethearts. That's tough. It broke my heart to learn there wasn't any Santa Claus.

There is a long list of people, up to and including the rank of major general, that I'd like to thank for their various kind deeds during the past months. But on the other hand, there are a lot of people I'd like to kick in the pants. We'll just call it square, except in the case of Staff Sergeant Dick Hanley (Richard), Sergeant Don E. Brewer (who posed—physically, not spiritually—for the character Herman), Major Ted Wagner, Major Jimmy Hungate, and Lieutenant John Lenahan, U.S.N.R. Their contributions, of a more practical nature generally than the usual "helpful advice and criticism," were and will always be appreciated.

To BE PERFECTLY FRANK, these first chapters may strike you as something less than hilarious. As a matter of fact about the time you reach page ten, you may knock off and lock your younger daughters in the coal bin.

Having thus hung out the "Adults Only" sign—from what I've seen in front of fourth-rate movie marquees, a surefire method of packin' 'em in—we'll start the feature.

June 29, 1943, looms up bigger to me than my sixth birthday, when I got a *two*-wheeler. That was the day I was suddenly yanked from the rigors of Army life and transferred to what the memoranda called a "Southwest Pacific Area Services Publication." Coming in the middle of a particularly rigid spell of particularly rigid training and following a slight misunderstanding between a colonel and myself, this transfer left me happier than a novice with his first reefer. It was effective immediately. Or, as my orders so quaintly put it, "EM WP without delay via auth Govt rail T to proper sta and orgn, reporting o/a for dy." Translated: "Enlisted man will pro-

ceed without delay via authorized Government rail transportation to proper station and organization, reporting on arrival for duty."

See? That wasn't so hard.

I packed hurriedly under the very close scrutiny of my three dearest friends, who had been nursing for some weeks a fairly valid suspicion that I was bribing our laundry girl (with Camay soap and American matches) to mark all our clothes "st geo." I then proceeded with no more delay than might be expected—considering the necessity of rescuing my other pants from the clutches of a notoriously unhurried cleaning establishment, the intricasies of the Army Rail Transportation Office and the perennial shortage of rolling stock. Following twenty-four hours in a second-class compartment with three submarine sailors and the high points of their last patrol, and the low points of their last liberty, I detrained in what is generally considered in these parts as "the bes' damn town in Australia, maybe the world."

The underseas contingent yelled a hasty farewell and disappeared screaming "Taxi!" I stood around on the platform waiting for an RAAF contingent to finish mauling the baggage. Waiting with me were two other Yanks: one large, one small. We became acquainted in no time and fast friends about thirty seconds later, when it de-

3

veloped that they, too, were proceeding without delay to the same sta and orgn I was.

They'd come from somewhat farther afield than I, and had been proceeding via auth Govt rail T for a matter of days. So they were even grimier than I was. Having slept in our clothes and dispensed with shaving because of the usual lack of water and the high-road-to-hell nature of the track, none of us at first glance would have passed for the pick of the Southwest Pacific.

The large one looked like W. C. Fields and said his name was Herman; the squat one was Max. Collecting our baggage—three loosely packed, faded blue barracks bags that hamstrung our lives during our trek up the platform like the three witches which hamstrung Macbeth's—we checked most of it, snatched a cab from under the nose of a frail old frail (our life in the Army has made us self-reliant), piled in, and directed the driver to our proper sta that we might report for dy.

Dy, we found, was an eight-to-five affair on the fifth floor of a building located in the heart of the downtown metropolitan district. We would be quartered for the time being at Warwick Farm, a camp with a 1:30 A.M. bed check and a 6:30 A.M. roll call. Between 5:00 in the afternoon and 1:30 and 6:30 and 8:00 A.M. we were as free as the breeze. Dy would begin the following morning.

Going across the street to headquarters, we threaded our way through eight floors full of assorted Army, Navy and Air Corps brass, American Red Cross personnel, civilian secretaries on their way to tea, and soldiers looking for the finance department. Eventually we found the Commandant's office, went in, and were subjected to the usual rigmarole of name, rank and serial number necessarily connected with a change of sta.

While we were waiting for the clerk to soak up the significant data and type our Class A passes, a soldier came in, spotted us and

introduced himself as another pick of the Southwest Pacific. Our Class A's completed and in our hot little hands, he hustled us outside, backed us into a corner and unfolded an amazing tale.

He was, he confided, a soldier of some experience. Of our camp he said, "You don't wanna stay at *Warwick!* It's twenty miles out of town, in a marsh, and it's colder than hell. We call it Happy Valley. Takes you forty-five minutes t' get there by train an' that's a special. It's a four-mile walk from the tram line. You don't wanna stay *there*. But look (and backing us farther into our corner, he lowered his voice like a man discussing his best friend's bankruptcy) I hear we're gonna get *per diem*. Now so long as you don't go out to the Valley an' report in, the Commandant won't know you're supposed to be there. They never check up. Once yu' go out an' report, though, you're stuck. They got a board with tags on it, an' yu' gotta pick your tag off every morning at breakfast or they restrict yu' for a week. I'm restricted right now."

We wavered a minute, then unanimously agreed that what he said was probably true: Our lives would be complete without the tags of Happy Valley. Besides, we assured each other, "If they never check up . . ."

Adjourned to a pub around the corner (we were just standing in the crush of humanity that lined the bar, hoping for the physical or financial collapse of some of those in front) we discussed our present sta. We were, we decided, all in all, just about as close to civilian life as we could hope to come and still retain our franking privileges. Practically speaking, we were out of the Army. OUT OF THE ARMY! My God. What we did in the ensuing days—or daze—is generally known as going off the deep end.

And why did we thus plunge in with all the buoyancy of a sack of cement? No more reveilles and no more taps. No more bran-headed N.C.O.'s. No more nincompoop ninety-day wonders. No more details and no more latrines to dig, scrub, move and screen. No more, no more, no more.

We were "out." True, we were a long way from home. We had no loved ones to fly to. Loving ones, yes, but no loved ones. From what I've heard around and about, in sundry mess halls and through numerous mosquito bars, our views were held by quite a number of Johnnies in the A.U.S. Those Johnnies, honorably discharged and on their way home, will probably be just as wildly, deliriously, insanely happy as we were.

What follows could, I suppose, be instrumental in swinging public opinion toward a prolonged demobilization period. But the truth, man, that's what we're after.

You there, with the bangs and the all-day sucker, get along to Chapter IV.

The three of us—Herman, Max, and I—left the bar we'd never reached and stormed the city's leading hotel. Perhaps it was the gleam in our eye, perhaps Herman's words of honey to the desk girl, perhaps an evil fate: anyway, we got accommodations. A jaded, world-weary bell hop of fifteen, whom we promptly christened Buttons, manhandled our luggage into the lift; a World War I veteran, named Pop, carried ("whisked" is not the word in this case) us to the ninth floor; and Buttons guided us to our new-found castle in the air, Number 96.

Number 96 was tastefully decorated with two beds, double and single, a wardrobe, a carpet, hot and cold running water, a full-length mirror, a phone and a small sign: "Owing to the National Emergency the Management regrets that it is unable to serve tea in rooms." The least of our regrets, believe me. Flinging our belongings on the floor, we stormed off to the showers, down the hall, third on the left.

There, while removing the accumulation of two days' second-class travel, we carried on a shouted conversation: "Oh brother! What d'ya think of it? Jeez, a *hotel* room! An' hot showers! Boy, this is the life. Go t' bed when yu' want to. And where yu' want

8

to (that from Herman). Wait'll I tell the guys back in camp! It's like yu' dream about! How much dough yu' got? Eighteen pounds, how much you? Ten, but I can get a partial payment. Say, there's a bar, with stools, on the second floor. Yu' see that? No! yu' mean like at *home?* Yeah. Well, c'mon, less get down there! What time's it close? Buttons says six o'clock, but if you're a guest they serve till midnight. We're guests. *MIDNIGHT!* Oh brother!"

A mousy civilian character came out of the fourth shower at this point and favored us with a stare that made it pretty clear he had us pegged for three pilots, rescued after months of wandering in the hell of the Owen Stanleys, but wasn't condoning our behavior by any means.

A few minutes later we descended on the bar, like a horde of North Dakota locusts descending on a patch of Golden Hybrid. What Buttons had said was true: Non-guests were heisted away at six, but waving our room key like a magic wand, we stayed on and on. Until, around seven our confidential friend from Happy Valley showed up and suggested we ramble over to the local Non Coms Club where things were cheaper.

With us money was no object, but we strung along with our chaperone, whose name was George. This bit of heaven that the

Base Section NCO's called their own was located a few blocks away, directly across the street from the town's leading dance hall, "the Troc"—undeniably a handy location. A narrow structure of several stories, it had no distinguishing characteristics. Nevertheless, George found it unerringly. We promised to join, of course, and that, plus George's influence, got us inside. We were inclined to linger on the ground floor where half a dozen youngish Australian wenches served what may have been genuine hamburgers and a pretty fair brand of cross-counter repartee, but George pushed on, propelling us past a battery of honest-to-goodness pinball machines and up the stairs.

The second floor left us gasping for words with which to express our unbounded joy and amazement. A polished bar flanked one side, there was a carpet on the floor, chummy little tables, a murky lighting effect and a blaring juke-box. However, this retreat was for couples only and we weren't allowed to linger. Anyway, George was still urging us up the stairs.

On the third floor we found the club offices and the bottle department. We met the president, a dyspeptic master sergeant, who gave us a limp hand and a glassy stare, filled out our membership cards, planked a quid on the line, and immediately made use of the club's greatest privilege. From a surly character surrounded by more liquor than Herman or Max or I, fresh from the dry outback, knew existed, we purchased our weekly ration of one bottle each, then followed George, already plunging on up the stairs. If friend George had paused first and screamed "Excelsior!" we wouldn't have been much surprised.

The fourth floor was strictly gents. There was a battered bar presided over by a large flabby lady called "Mom," no carpet, some

scarred and battered tables, a juke of course, and four or five slot machines. We grabbed a table and George explained the merchandising system: First, we bought tickets from Mom, then from one of the . . . (I'm sorry, but *courtesans* has got to be the word) who slopped around behind the bar, we got our drinks. This system, George confided, had been put in shortly after the addition of civilian help had led to small but regular deficits where there should have been profits.

Over drinks we learned that there was still another floor, but presumably nobody ever lasted long enough to get up there. Later on we met a few of George's friends. Per Diem Commandos all, from

11

the tops of their impeccable Pershing caps to the tips of their shiny oxfords, they could gripe about all phases of the Army and the war just as well and as heartily as we could. Following a couple of hours' discussion on this fascinating topic and the two others that monopolize all Army round tables—Home and Women—George left to catch the Happy Valley special. Herman and Max and I discovered shortly that the day's thrills had left us three very tired boys. For months we'd been going to bed pretty regularly and seldom later than ten o'clock. We said good night and took a taxi back to our hotel, where Duttons, Pop, a hard-faced waiter, and two night porters steered us through the reefs and up to 96.

Herman had, during the course of the evening, made what might have been passes at half a dozen waitresses. He kept us awake for fifteen minutes while he transcribed "Irene B-6065," "Mae REgent 4472," "Doris B-9861," "Joan MAin 2019," and the cryptic message, "meet Sam at Lothes," from a damp crumpled napkin to the wall behind our phone. Ronnie and Jill, he mumbled as he turned off the light, didn't have phones, but could be reached across a gin sling between 2 P.M. and midnight, Monday through Saturday.

On that we went to sleep.

IN THE SUCCEEDING DAYS, duty occupied our little heads from eight till five. After five we occupied ourselves. Our town, nineteenth month after the American arrival, showed only a smattering of Yanks during the daytime. The center of things had moved to the north. Toward evening, however, or late in the P.M. if it was cloudy, several hundred furloughees crawled out of their beds and appeared on the streets, ready and eager to resume the strain of forgetting the strain they'd been under during months of duty in New Guinea or the Northern Territory.

Taking care of these men in a solicitous manner that in six days relieved them of six months accumulated pay appeared to be one of the principal industries. Ours was, in short, a "leave town," and it fairly reeked of the atmosphere so often advanced by us younger

15

element as an excuse for that anything-goes-you-only-live-once philosophy and generally spoken of by staid and steady elders as something akin to V.D.—Wartime. Our little group decided, with no basis other than our own enthusiasm, that it was "better'n Paris in 1918."

In our efforts to prove the complete truth of this we spent about four hours a day in bed and devoted the rest of our time, after five, to wallowing in the half-forgotten luxuries and indiscretions of "civilian life." We were considerably aided in our wallowings by John the Doorman, a stalwart old man looking not unlike George Washington, who had taken quite a liking to us. Going in or out of the hotel we always stopped for a short chat about the weather or the larcenous practices of the local cabbies, a subject on which John was an expert. Following such a palaver we'd hint that we were in the market for an evening's entertainment. John, whose voice from years of calling cabs and placating drunks had dwindled to a throaty rasp, a mere husk of a voice, would lean toward us, look cautiously over his shoulder, slide the back of one hand to his jaw line and whisper hoarsely through the corner of his mouth that a night's fun was all right, but if we valued our lives, limbs and financial standing for God's sake stay away from King's Cross. With or without any encouragement, he'd go on to croak the sordid details of the latest crime, violence, or fast fleecing handed some unsuspecting Yank who'd ventured into one of the district's notorious dives. We'd look suitably shocked, gape, gasp, and ask, "No-o! Say, where is that place?" Peering suspiciously into the shadows again, lest some shill be lurking about, John would part with the address and further detailed information that would have enabled a tenderfoot Scout to find the establishment's Gents' Room in a blizzard. Then he'd call a taxi from the stand, warn us again about King's Cross and the local cabbies, and off we'd go. To King's Cross, of course.

Thus our adventures would begin. And Herman had a penchant for adventure. Things just naturally happened to Herman. His approach to the feminine sex was like the flight of a rocket—the further he got, the faster he went. And he all but trailed smoke.

On one such occasion, just after dusk, Herman spotted a young lady standing in a doorway, swooped on her, uncorked his Adam's apple and poured forth a gush of persuasion. In the middle of which

a tall R.A.A.F. flight officer stepped through the door, took the girl
by the arm dragging her out of Herman's reach, and indicated that
he and she were friends of long standing. Herman allowed that he
preferred staying anyway, and might even be inclined to argue
about it. Max and I intervened and led him away before blows could
be struck, but he came under protest, muttering and mumbling to
himself that well hell the couple still didn't look married to HIM.
Discretion was not Herman's strong point.

On another occasion, having beaten the streets of King's Cross for several hours with no notable success, Herman wound up in the alley behind Irene's (B-6065) flat. Irene's sister had threatened to kill Herman the next time he showed his face on the premises, so looking before he leapt, Herman climbed on a box and peered through a slit in the curtain. Thus, a few moments later, a strolling MP found him.

Still another sorry episode began during our lunch hour. Wandering, ogling, down the sidewalk, Herman lamped a lovely slouched in the usual doorway. Coming in like a Focke-Wolf, he pulled up and breathed, "What's your name?"

"Thelma," said she, flashing a mouthful of teeth. The ensuing conversation, while undeniably dull from the standpoint of repartee, resulted in our agreeing to meet Thelma and two friends at seven sharp that night, "On the corner of King and William, in front of the milk bar."

Max and I were slow in getting started that evening, and we never did catch up with Herman and his Thelma.

But pulling into 96 at eleven o'clock, whom should we find in bed? Well, Herman, of course. An utterly disconsolate, inconsolable, woebegone Herman. Asking after the charming Thelma, we got only grunts.

We laughed callously. Herman rolled over and refused to speak further.

But next day, Heaven help us, he was his horrible old self again. Max was wolfing alone that night, so come five o'clock, Herman and I had supper, then went up to "Joe's room." Joe, another Southwest Pacific pick, wasn't home himself, but in line with a fine humanitarian impulse about helping out with the housing shortage, he'd passed the word around that his room would be vacant for the evening. Four of us and two total strangers who'd somehow gotten wind of the situation showed up and took over. A shortage of the fairer sex was immediately noticeable, but soon remedied. Herman and I went out to beat the streets, returning in about twenty-five minutes with two charming creatures who appeared somewhat less charming inside in the light. So much so, in fact, that Herman immediately suggested we scuttle the ship and go back to the streets.

We did. And promptly met two more charming creatures, under a lamp post. Leering at them, Herman asked would they like to go someplace? The girls modestly suggested Ciro's might be nice. Well, for all we knew Ciro's was an opium den or maybe even a branch of the public library, but we hailed a cab, piled in, and were off.

Like all the other places we ever went to in a cab, Ciro's was to hell and gone out in the sticks, but almost worth the trip, Herman and I decided, for Ciro's was closer to the real thing in Stateside night clubs than either of us had seen for many a day. Somewhat larger than a piano crate, it housed a checkroom containing a saucy wench, a foyer like a hat box, tables, and a tiny space too crowded for dancing. The lights were suitably dim through the requisite amount of cigarette smoke. There was an orchestra stand, too, but as this was Sunday, the orchestra's holiday, a juke box, slugged stead-

ily with thrupences, provided the necessary pulsating background. Above all, as we discovered soon enough, the prices were Stateside, easily onto a par with the kind of financial rape we'd once been accustomed to. And paying the equivalent of three rocks for an inferior plate of chicken sandwiches left us practically dripping nostaglia as sad and as beautiful as any Spanish moss.

Only one thing was missing. There was no headwaiter. Instead, we supposed, there was a service star in the manager's office. On the floor a large matronly woman in black silk and a white lace apron guided us through the tables and the murk to a spot so delightfully near the juke that its blarings literally shivered the glassware.

Ciro's clientelle was about fifty-fifty U.S. Army and A.I.F. brass, and gay, over-age civilians, with here and there an Air Corps sergeant or a chief petty officer upholding the reputations of their respective services. The greater share were accompanied by the kind of well-dressed women generously described as "hard faced." Herman and I, wearing the clothes we'd hit town in (what with the press of sociability we'd run aground on since, we'd never found or taken the time to get our baggage out of hock) stood apart from the others like two plucked chickens in a peacock farm. Not that it bothered us any. We were still laboring along under our illusion about being out of the Army, and still too wildly, deliriously, and insanely happy to much care whether we'd come in tuxedos, grimy O.D.'s, or barrels and garters. Besides, our companions were certainly as hard faced as anybody's.

So Herman and I were nonchalant, and we nonchalantly parted with three quid ten for the chicken sandwiches and a bottle of gin. Half way through the latter Herman leaned across the table, with an ugly smirk, and whispered into his charming creature's shell-like ear. Whatever it was she immediately suggested that she and I dance, and literally hauled me to my feet and onto the floor. There, we were slowly ground to bits.

Herman, seasoned campaigner that he was, decided we must work a switch. We did, quietly, efficiently, and diplomatically, and the evening wore on. And a very wearing evening it was, too. The prize package I'd got managed to consume considerably more than her share of the gin, and she was, she told me, "simply *mad* about dancing, specially jitterbugging!" Well, whatever else I may or may

22

not be, I am *not* a jitterburg. All of which I scarcely had the breath
to mention, what with Blondie, who was bigger than I was, using
my body as a means of cutting a swath through the other dancers.
I've had rougher evenings perhaps, but on those occasions there was
at least some kind of official on hand to call fouls. Not so Ciro's.

Herman, in the meantime, playing his favorite roll of Big Man
Just off the Campus, laid in a further supply of chicken and grog
with a truly grandiose contempt of cost. Or so it seemed to me, and
I said so. Herman only laughed at that; actually, he let me know,
he was being pretty damned cagy about pouring my money down
the cash register. He'd found, following a close perusal of the wine
list while he could still see, that champagne was ten bob a bottle
cheaper than gin. Obviously a saving of ten bob on every purchase
of champagne. While Blondie was flinging me gaily about the juke
box, he'd saved us thirty bob. Under ordinary circumstances I might
have argued with Herman. But how could I worry? Instead of a
precious pass that expired at midnight, a thirty-mile ride in a drafty
GI truck, four hours' sleep, and a miserable reveille looming up
like a thunderhead on my limited horizon, I could look forward to

No. 96, a feather bed, no reveille whatsoever and, mayhap on the following evening, Ciro's.

I didn't, and Herman saved us another ten bob, and then, just to show the girls *he* was no piker—a fact that seemed to me quite self-evident—he lit a cigarette with a flourish and a pound note. "Jush as a geshure," he said. While I could scarcely look upon myself as any kind of miser at the time, still his gesture sobered me like an ice-pack.

I skipped out, however, and hailed a cab. In it, the girls let us know that the next stop would home for them. So home it was, we later computing, from the look of the meter, that both resided in Perth.

In bed, finally, tired but something short of happy, Herman asked me, "What was yours' name?"

"Laura," I told him.

"Mmmm," said Herman, and after a pause, "Laura what?"

"Russell, she said."

"Mmmm!" said Herman, with considerably more feeling than before, "That's what mine told me too. . . ."

Now PER DIEM is the dream of many a varicose colonel. But, though many are called, few are paid; and, generally speaking, enlisted men drawing full per diem are rarer than tattooed WACs. However, in view of the peculiar nature of our duties and the responsibility of rationing and quartering such happy-go-lucky soldiers, the powers authorized for us per diem. We learned of this one morning a few days after our encounter with the swarms of Laura Russells, and a very happy forenoon it was. Some rapid calculation showed us that in addition to our regular pay (a negligible sum) we would receive approximately $150 a month, or considerably more than most of us had ever earned before.

It was true, of course, that our per-diem status made us the very basest kind of Base Section Commandos. Base Section Commandos, incidentally, could perhaps do with a word of explanation. In the E.T.O. they're known, I believe, as Piccadilly Commandos; in the

Mediterranean as Casablanca Commandos; we, for that matter, were also known as S.O.S. (Services of Supply) Commandos, Grace Building Commandos, and a host of unprintable names, among them "damn pasty-faced town soldiers."

Now base sections are an integral part of the Army Service Force, each administering the supply needs of a designated area, and thus, naturally enough, usually stationed in the area's largest city. Comparatively speaking, theirs is a soft life, and even a confirmed base-section boy, with the weight of the war on his back and a four-foot file of unfilled requisitions as his direct responsibility, pinned down, will admit as much. These pasty faces, handling nothing more lethal than a 14-inch–carriage Remington, are hated and despised. And envied.

Having envied and despised a number of base sections ourselves for months, we learned of our per diem and stepped across the line. We knew what kind of schlemiels we'd become when we did it; we'd been telling our friends, by candlelight in a lonesome tent, just what we thought of Base Section Commandos for, in some cases, years. As of the instant our O.I.C. (officer-in-charge) said, "Well, boys, I got you per diem," we became singularly unimpressed with those views. In fact, on learning we were per-diem boys and dyed-in-the-wool Warwick Commandos, we were fit to celebrate another Armistice.

We'd evidently envied more than we'd despised. Nor was our rejoicing in any way dampened by the fact that our per diem wouldn't actually become effective until the first of the following month. In the meantime, we felt confident, we could live in hopes instead of in Happy Valley.

Before the day was over this decision was open to considerable question. At noon, going out to lunch, Max and I discovered that between the three of us we had something less than three quid. It was then 12:30, July 5th (the 4th having passed without incident). A drastic cut in overhead was obviously in order. Accordingly, we ate a frugal lunch, and back in 96 phoned the desk for our bill. Five pound ten, they told us. We answered with a short gasp; hung up; and, stretched on our beds, discussed the situation.

"Well," said Herman, fifteen minutes of desultory conversation having brought forth no solution to speak of, "I'm goin' to get one

27

more hot shave out of this hostelry anyway." Lumbering to the wash stand, he did. I availed myself of one more glance at the daily paper said hostelry provided. Max, more practical, sat considering the handwriting on the wall, and, still practical, presently copied that handwriting down in his little black book (Irene B-6065, Mae REgent 4472, Doris B-9861, etc.). We left the hotel and went back to the office, whistling.

Next day we invested the remainder of the three quid in one last steak dinner, then went into the loan business. Two here, three there, ten bob from the telephone girl (Ella, dial 0)—Herman's contribution—and we were able to pay the damages on 96; which, by that time, had climbed to eight pounds even.

Our departure from that hospitable establishment was scarcely a thing of glory. Loaded to the gunwales, burdened with our faded blue barracks bags, sundry miscellaneous packs and boxes, and a dirty white laundry sack, we trundled through the lobby. Herman's overcoat bulged with stolen towels and a monogrammed pillowcase to make up for months of sleeping on a camp cot. In addition, with one hand he clutched to his heart a bedraggled mess of dirty laundry and, in the other, a giant-size can of foot powder.

Still, from force of a short few days habit, we hailed a cab. And found we had but two bob, and were forced to wave it away, empty. Herman dropped his laundry at this point and had to scrabble for it on his hands and knees. His foot powder rolled into the gutter. When we asked John about a tram, he only pointed, silently, eloquently. The crowning blow.

We slept at the American Red Cross that night, between sailors coming in and waking up a buddy to regale him, in loud whispers, with lurid tales of his evening at the Trocadero. The next day brought a reprieve in the form of a money order for ten quid, long owed me by a soldier who, finding himself in New Guinea and therefore desperate for a means of spending money, paid it back. Redeeming the order for ready scratch, we forcibly prevented Herman from sinking his share in grog and decided to look for a room.

Naturally, we looked in King's Cross, or as we'd learned to call it by then, "the dirty half mile." We began our search that evening; and came away with two rooms. Next day we induced another pick of the Southwest Pacific, name of Jackson, to come in with us.

Our private residence, or at any rate that part of it shared by Herman and me, consisted of a small room containing two broken beds, a battered wardrobe, and a deal of gracefully peeling wallpaper. There was a kitchenette too, so small that Herman, who hit 210, went in sideways and backed out. The kitchenette boasted an ancient gas jet that went out regularly and had to be revived with penny offerings, a sparse and heterogeneous collection of outmoded

kitchenware, a bird cage, and a single dirty window that opened
with difficulty on an inspiring view of alley, garbage cans, and third
floor backs. The bird cage, we presently learned, was intended not
as a rookery but as a larder. Suspended as it was, swinging freely in
midair, it more or less discouraged raids on the part of the other
inhabitants of our residence, of which there were many, most of
whom scampered rather than crawled.

We learned too, and soon, that our residence was not to be as
private as we had imagined. Within three minutes of our arrival, a
bouncing blonde appeared in the doorway, hitched one hand onto
her hips in the manner of a slightly punchy Mae West, and said,
"Hello, gotta cigarette? I'm Hazel."

Further conversation that first evening disclosed that Hazel was a welder, the wife of an R.A.A.F. flight sergeant at present home on leave. Hers was a free and generous nature; and, as an added attraction, a heart of gold beat beneath her prominent bosom. When she learned that we were not only destitute but starving, a fact that Herman and I kept plugging at every opportunity, she insisted nothing would do but that we should come over and share her tea. We did, "share" being scarcely the word for what we did to Hazel's tea.

We grew increasingly lean and gaunt and hungry. Rumors of Happy Valley's serving the best GI food in the Southwest Pacific were now filtering through. At the end of a week, with a bare quid between us and Happy Valley, we held another council of war. The problems of civilian life had begun to burn in and it was rather a serious affair. Max and I had about conceded that self-preservation was strongest of the instincts (next to strongest, anyway), and we cast two halting votes for the Valley, but Herman saved the day by suggesting we move our clothes to the office and ourselves back to the American Red Cross. Following Herman's suggestion, we lived for several days in the approved tradition of "The Front Page," shaving in the men's room at the office, storing socks and dirty shirts in various drawers, and whiling away our evenings as best we could, considering that we had no home, only beds. As a matter of fact, our having beds was somewhat illegal, as the American Red Cross was supposedly reserved for the exclusive use of soldiers on furlough, but by brazenly forging APO's, units and organizations, we beat this rap.

Thus began an existence which, in retrospect, I can compare with nothing so much as the drunken lurchings of a clown riding a unicycle.

To begin with, shortly after we returned to the Red Cross, Max dug up an old friend of his in the Graves Registration Bureau (a live one, I might add) and worked him for the loan of a five. Herman and I never met this friend; Max guarded him as jealously as though he were the Comstock Lode, which, as far as Max was concerned, he was. A few days later, realizing that Herman and I were quite content to live off his strike anyway, sight unseen if need be, Max withdrew from our little partnership. This left Herman and me back on the rocks, to leeward, with breakers ahead and a gale blowing up. Our credit was practically exhausted too.

32

Still we clung to our "civilian life." Our expenses, actually, were rather slim: two quid a week for our N.C.O.-club grog ration (a triple-A priority we gave that), one and six (25 cents) per day for beds, what was left over, if there was any left over, we put in food, mostly tea and grilled cheese sandwiches.

Haircuts, something that, during our service with troops, we'd often gotten just to while away an afternoon, were hopelessly out of our reach, there being no lady barbers, but by turning up our collars and scrunching down, we got by. Nor were we above riding trams for free if the opportunity presented itself.

Great teacher that experience is, I learned, during those eight or ten days while we lived mostly on hope, something I had almost never given any thought to before—the art of small talk. Herman, of course, was quite adept at this himself; under his guidance and through necessity, I became reasonably adept myself at discussing the weather, the war, and the shortage of grog. I practiced daily on the character who ran our lift.

But two growing boys can't live on six beers a day. Consequently, we looked around for something more in the way of good solid food. We found it the following Sunday afternoon while visiting the beach. Just exactly why we visited the beach I don't remember. Anyway, we arrived, picked our way through the crowd; and strolled among the innumerable young ladies sprawled on the sand. The bathers were soaking up the sun, eating, reading, sleeping, arguing, and all cursing Herman and me as we kicked sand in their faces. We all but trampled one old lady into the gravel, and with that gave up trying to watch every girl on the beach, sat down, and settled for those traveling east to west.

The old lady, none the worse for her experience—and it must have been an experience, Herman wore a size of 12—asked us, presently, how long had we been in Australia? Catching ourselves in the nick of time, we stifled the usual, built-to-Government-specifications answer—"Too long!"—and told her fifteen months. She said my that was a long time, and went on to say that she had a nephew, A.I.F., who had been overseas four years now. We said my that *was* a long time. Herman caught my eye at this point. I nodded "roger," said something sparkling like, "My, this certainly is a nice beach," Herman followed with more praise of the locale, and from there on in we played that old lady like two Izaak Waltons hooking one of his trouts. Properly netted in about twenty minutes, she asked would we like to come up for tea someday? I heaved a long sigh; Herman wiped the saliva off his chin and, pinning her shoulders to the sand, screamed, "Yes! Tuesday?" The old lady said yes, Tuesday would be fine; we produced paper and pencil like two talent scouts signing the Panther Woman, took her name and address and flat number, and left her reeling under a smother of hasty, though polite, goodbyes.

Withdrawing a few yards, we congratulated each other madly and discussed, wonderingly, almost gloatingly, the great new field of possibilities thus opened to us. Visions of tea and scones and tarts danced before our eyes.

We forged ahead, still dripping charm but mindful of Herman's feet, and during the course of the afternoon signed up seven teas and one dinner date, on Sunday week. Three of these invitations, as luck would have it, were for Tuesday; and, while that seemed a lot of tea,

34

we could scarcely ask Mrs. Millicent Dougherty, Mrs. John Hogan, and Mrs. Percy Purvis to rearrange their week's engagements just for us. Instead we scheduled Dougherty at five-thirty, Hogan at seven, Purvis for a late snack at eight-fifteen, and hoped the over-burdened tram system wouldn't fail us. Though we went to bed hungry that night, somehow it didn't bother us much.

The week that followed lives on in my memory as a very bad dream indeed, being naught but a sweet wet blur of tea—black, white, green, and orange pekoe; scones—hot, cold, and indifferent; tarts—delicious, edible, and otherwise; ham; green tomatoes; discol-ored family albums; uncomfortable chairs; stuffy parlors; morose canaries; long cold tram rides; doorbells; wrong addresses; and in-numerable vague, shadowy introductions. We did, of course, in our mad wet whirl, meet some fairly delectable sisters, daughters, and friends, all of whom I would gladly have recognized anywhere. But being financially embarrassed to the point of wincing everytime we heard a cash register ring, these meetings led to little or nothing, generally nothing.

During the course of the week we received four offers of re-turn engagements; but, lacking Tuesday and Thursday, we took to the beach again on the following Sunday, after a dinner of inferior duck. Our hearts, we found, weren't in it. All we signed up were two tea jobs; and, though we tried to fill them, it was no use. Our stomachs rebelled.

On Monday P.M., at Mrs. Purvis' again, we cracked. Herman, in plain view of Mrs. Purvis, gagged over a cup of her very best, squirted a small, orange-pekoe geyser over her favorite potted plant, dropped a handful of jam tarts on the rug, and staggered toward the door, gasping, "Sick! Air!" While Mrs. Purvis revived the gerani-ums, I slyly deposited my own tea over a rubber plant, excused my-self (I somehow felt that a little air might do me no harm either), and went after Herman.

We canceled the remainder of our invitations by simply not show-ing up and went back to reaming small change out of the rest of the staff. "Civilian life" by this time had become something of a night-mare and too much like *The Grapes of Wrath* to be really enjoyed, but still we clung to it, living on hope and tap water, and clutching at the occasional ten-bob notes that fluttered past us, like two tor-

pedoed members of the Merchant Marine might clutch at any flying fish nearing their life raft. One by one the other members of the staff broke, sighed, and checked in at Happy Valley; but Herman and I hung on, unchecked, untagged, *free!* These other members, as they grew fat and rested, tortured us with tales of four eggs for breakfast, hotcakes with butter, fried chicken, and pork chops.

But two growing boys can't live on tap water, no matter what the quantity, so again we slashed expenses. And a neat trick it was, too, our only expenses being what we spent on food and shelter. As further slashing of the former would have had much the same effect as would slashing our wrists with a dull razor, we necessarily turned to the problem of shelter. For about a week this had consisted of half a double-decker bed apiece, at the American Red Cross Service Club; price, ninepence. There were a couple of minor disadvantages.

One disadvantage showed up at 7:30 in the persons of half a dozen decrepit ladies lugging brooms, and mops and cackling get up, they had to mike the beds right aw'y. Most of the time, I must admit, it was just as well that I dragged myself out of bed and stumbled away then. Duty, after all, began at eight.

Now and then, by snarling and swearing and refusing to come out from beneath the covers, we could stave off the boskies until say eight-thirty, but sooner or later they closed in on us, remorseless as quicksand, reared their faces cobra-like over the edge of our beds, and hissed the one about getting them mide right aw'y.

On the 14th of July (Bastile Day, though I didn't remember it at the time) Herman and I were in a fair way to go storming the homes of the aristocrats ourselves, screaming, "Bread!" That was the day we ran out of money at three in the afternoon, had two bananas and a considerable amount of tap water for supper, and blew into the Red Cross at 10 P.M., with no beds and no ninepence, but some vague hopes of concluding a little deal wherein a pint of blood might be involved. (We figured we had about a pint of thin, watery blood to spare, between us.) Nobody made us an offer.

At five that afternoon we took the plunge. We tried to pawn something, anything. Seeking out our old friend, John the Door-man, who, once assured we weren't looking for rooms, stopped treating us like the old bag-and-rag men we must have looked and was only too glad to tell us where and which way. Off we went, following John's directions, until several tawdry ladies greeted us with "Hello-o boys . . . .?" and a number of small rickety signs assured us that within the district money was being loaned—nay, given away —at ludicrously low rates of interest, say 150 per cent.

After a couple of false starts we slipped down an alley and through a door bearing a small sign: "Valuables Exchanged." It was the first time either of us had ever had anything to do with pawnshops and we were perhaps strangely but nonetheless so thoroughly embarrassed that when the proprietor, a wrinkled old grandma of unmistakably Gypsy blood, squeaked "Yes?" we muffed our lines like a couple of small-time politicos making their first network appearance. Herman finally stuttered that we were just looking around, which was a damn lie. And Grandma, with perhaps eighty-eight years experience in the "loan" business behind her, very well knew that it was a damn lie. Guessing correctly that whatever else we might have in mind, we had no hot ice for sale, she took herself off, muttering under her breath, and sent in a substitute for the likes of us. This character, a youth of maybe nineteen, wearing pimples and a dirty blue shirt, still had about forty years experience on Herman and me; and, when we at last got it out that the purpose of our visit concerned a watch, he said shortly, "Lemme see it." We handed him my broken Elgin, he scrutinized it, briefly, and promptly pronounced it worthless. "Does 'er run?" he asked.

Well, no, we had to admit, it didn't run, but the parts . . . ?

"Nuh-uh," said Pimples. "We carn't use no parts." Though his attitude left us feeling that we must already owe *him* something for his time and trouble, we persisted. We argued that, running or not, busted or otherwise, since it had cost eight quid new (stretching it a bit) it must still be worth *something*.

Pimples said, "Gotta smoke?" and, when we'd lit him up, condescended to give my Elgin another suspicious going over. Whatever it was he saw left him aghast at our cupidity; but, his naturally generous nature overwhelming him, he leaned toward us and said in

a low voice, "The ole bitch'll skin me f' it, but I could give yu' two bob."

The difference between an original investment of $17.50 and the equivalent of 32 cents was too much, even for Herman and me. Besides, the anger that welled up in us was almost as filling as a plate of fish and chips. We said nuts, give us back the watch. Pimples passed it over, his actions indicating that, man of the world that he was, he could survive our outrageous lack of gratitude and, business man that he was, could also survive our quietly collapsing of starvation right there on his counter, though he would have preferred we first get off the premises. We left, muttering something about taking our watch someplace else.

Tomorrow we would go to Happy Valley. And enlist.

Being hungrier than ever, what with having nothing under our belts for breakfast but tap water, we were still pretty sold on becoming Happy Valleyites as soon as possible all next day. As it turned out it was just as well. Shortly before dinner one of the staff, a rather ordinary pick of the Southwest Pacific, stopped by my desk and said, "Would you like to get ten pounds out of the Red Cross?" A coherent reply was beyond me, but he gathered from the way I worked my mouth and clutched at the air with my thin hands that yes, I'd like very much to get ten pounds out of the Red Cross or anybody else. Accordingly, he wrote my name on a piece of paper (I noted it read like the staff roster) and went on to the next desk. For a few minutes I dreamed dreams in which ten quid played a prominent part, but thinking of anything except food was an effort, and visions of the reputedly substantial diet served at Happy Valley presently pushed the ten quid out of the picture. As I say, it was just as well.

Our friend with the roster stormed the Red Cross immediately after lunch. He returned in about twenty minutes looking fairly wretched and accompanied by two Red Cross officials. All three stalked through the office with never a glance at the rest of us and

disappeared into the room occupied by our O.I.C. Who presently stuck his head through the door and called Herman and me by our rank and last names, an ominous sign. The instructions he gave us, once we were inside, were short and to the point: we would report to the commandant at Camp Warwick at six that evening, so help us God. We refrained from telling him that we were, perhaps, a couple of jumps ahead of him, said "Yes sir!" and withdrew, casting venomous glances at our alleged friend.

Just exactly what had transpired between this friend and the Red Cross was pretty much of a deep secret for a long time, but eventually, word by awful word, the inside story of the whole fiasco leaked out. In the end it shaped up something like this: our friend, blithely walking in on the Red Cross equivalent of two majors, had just as blithely requested a loan of eighty pounds, or something more than the Red Cross was in the habit of loaning, just like that. So they questioned him rather closely regarding why he needed eighty pounds. Our friend, who had apparently been blundering along through life with some pretty vague ideas on how the Red Cross operates, became confused, put both feet in his mouth, and stuttered generally until all concerned (two staff assistants and a club director had been called in by that time) were pretty well convinced that our friend intended establishing a buzzing little white-slave traffic. And with *their* eighty pounds! They "investigated." It was the investigation that brought to light Herman's and my unexplained absence from the Happy Valley roster and, in a coldly logical sequence, led to our joining the Happy Valley roster, as of six that evening. Thus it was that we said good-by to our civilian life, without regret, and, accompanied by our faithful barracks bags, showed up as directed at the Pitt Street station at 5:15 sharp and boarded the Happy Valley special.

We were received like very ordinary GI's indeed, not criminals. A bored lieutenant, warming his hands at the stove, told an equally bored sergeant to assign us a tent; the sergeant passed the buck to a corporal who, spotting a private slipping out the door, yelled, "Hey, Mickey, fix these guys up with beds and stuff." Mickey, trapped, came back; dug out a book; asked us our names, ranks, serial numbers, and organization; and told us we would sleep in row 6, tent 19,

beds 1 and 4. He told us too, "Yu' can get yu' blankets in the supply room, which is right next door. The woodpile is behind the mess hall. Chow is now."

Herman and I, hearing that, literally clawed our way into our barracks bags, yanked out our messkits, and plunged into the night and the chow line. We were back in the groove. And our first meal at Happy Valley, insofar as we were concerned, undoubtedly consisted of some of the best GI food ever served in the Southwest Pacific Area. We ate until we hurt.

Our financial condition continued poor, but at least we were eating and sleeping. You'd be amazed at what a help that can be. We even admitted in the privacy of the men's toilet that, had we but known, we would have enlisted sooner. To hell with civilian life.

I LEFT THE BEST damn city in Australia within a few weeks of succumbing to the dietetic wonders of Happy Valley. In all truth, saying good-by to Herman, the kind of chow the Valley featured, and the free and easy companionship of the Dirty Half Mile were somewhat saddening, but the hurry and worry of packing and fighting my way through the Transportation Corps left little time for tearful farewells. Then too, it was the first time since "joining" the A.U.S. that I'd been allowed to travel more than thirty miles without being counted, checked, double-checked, and inspected half to death at intervals along the way.

This time I was on my own; and safely tucked away between my shirt and me were my orders, a thick sheaf of carbon copies that promised considerable in the way of travel, listing a number of APO's, and winding up, in their own quaint way, "and such other places in New Guinea and the Islands as may be deemed necessary for the completion of instructions of CG [Commanding General]." My orders arranged for my eventual return in a sentence reading: "On completion TD [temporary duty] EM will return pro orgn &

sta," and gibbered too, "FD auth pay MALR TCNT TDN," which meant that the Finance Department of the U.S. Army, properly approached with a sufficient number of copies of my orders, would break down and pay me a monetary allowance in lieu of rations; that the Transportation Corps of the U.S. Army would furnish me "necessary transportation"; and that "transportation [was] deemed necessary." The final sentence, if it was a sentence, read: "1-5600 P 432-02 03 A 0425-24," for all I knew, the Adjutant General's equivalent of "now is the time for all good men . . ."

Admittedly a fair share of my orders looked like nothing so much as typographical errors, but somewhere along the line of my Army career I'd heard an experienced lieutenant colonel say, "Son, never travel in the Army without some kind of a piece of paper, with your name on it," and I knew that the flimsies tickling my stomach would be of considerably more value to me than my pants or the power of speech. I guarded them with my life.

Said orders had popped into the office early that morning and been distributed to the three of us who were going, as it was laughingly called, "into the field," by our O.I.C., with instructions to arrange our transportation. The three of us, Joe, The Professor and I, had left our desks and gone to the Transportation Corps, where, on producing our orders and convincing a suspicious staff-sergeant that they were bona fide and not, after all, blatant forgeries (he didn't actually *say* they were blatant forgeries), we were given small, greenish slips of paper, not unlike checks, that certified we were traveling "on Government business," at a cost of ten pounds, five-and-six to U.S. taxpayers. Joe's, in addition, stated that he, being a first-three-grader, was entitled to the relative privacy and comfort of a first-class compartment. I, as usual, and The Professor, who was likewise well below the first three grades, would travel second class. In return for all this the Transportation Corps kept one copy of our orders.

Now The Professor was another pick of the Southwest Pacific and had, from the first, distinguished himself as a character. Short to the point of dumpiness, with a beery, battered complexion considerably the worse for too much cheap wine, his personality at first contact was much like that of a day-old doughnut. His eyes were badly bloodshot and seldom more than a quarter open, in all a good basis for Herman's contention that he looked like a mole. Still, The Professor had his points. He suffered acutely from the cold; but, no slave to convention, he fought the chill tooth and nail, regardless of appearance, and wore constantly and without buttoning it an over-coat several sizes too large for him, an overseas cap of the same cut, and a long, olive-brown muffler with tassled ends that trailed behind him in the breeze or hung limply down his front

At the time of our leaving, the cold and the cheap wine had caught up with The Professor, and he was suffering an acute though tem-porary loss of voice. Throughout the day, as we ran ourselves ragged collecting our transportation, baggage, clothes, laundry, a bottle or so of grog, and a part of the money that was owed The Professor, he kept pawing at my arm, rasping and gasping, at in-tervals, "Haaaswk aaaaaark gosss aaaatch," like a persistent though somewhat discouraged spook. Eventually, along about three in the afternoon, I gathered that he was asking for a light. After that he had only to produce a cigarette and wave it hopefully and I would give him a light, thus working a considerable saving on his taut vocal cords.

Joe left at seven that night, on the first division of the "mile trine." The Professor and I left an hour later on the second division. Her-man, who was (and is, I fear) a Base Section Commando at heart, came down to see me off, didn't deign to get out of his taxi, promised faithfully that he would forward my laundry as soon as it was ready (ten months later I presume it still isn't ready), and left to keep his second date of the evening.

The Professor hove in sight a few minutes after Herman left, lugging a large brown pasteboard suitcase he had somewhere acquired, the usual barracks bag, and a girl. This light of his life he had met, he rasped, either that night or the night before, I didn't quite catch which, though from their actions I would have guessed they'd met years ago. Her name was Ethel or Beryl or something like that. I rather than The Professor still would have gotten any stares that were being passed around the station, simply because I had neglected to bring any girl at all. The station, as always, was crowded with the soldiers, sailors, and air corps of two nations, practically all of whom had dug up or bribed or gotten the loan of a body—wife, sister, mother, sweetheart, acquaintance or what-have-you—and brought it down to the station to see them leave or arrive as the case might be. Many, particularly the sailors, had several bodies clinging to their arms and necks, and there were, no doubt, a number of couples who, as in the story, had just come down for the necking and to hell with the trains.

The Professor and I, with Ethel (or Beryl) trailing us, found the U.S. Army R.T.O.; had our little green slips checked, stamped, signed, etc. by a surprisingly civil sergeant; then recrossed the length of the station and lined up at the ticket windows, where, after standing in line for perhaps fifteen minutes, we were given small orange pasteboard tickets in exchange for our little green slips, which, by that time, were wearing a pretty-well-worked-over appearance. The second division of the "mile trine," the ticket man told us, was due to leave from track 6 around 8:05. We carried part of our luggage to the baggage office and delivered it to an obvious mental case who marked it with some kind of coded scrawl and gave us two blue checks. When we asked him, he assured us it would go north on the same train we were going on, then asked, us as an afterthought, what train we were going on? As it appeared highly improbable that we would ever see them again, we took a last fond look at our barracks bags, then wandered over to track 6, found the second division, car 13, compartment 8, seats 57 and 58, trundled inside and settled ourselves.

While we waited for the engineer's railroad watch to reach 8:05 or thereabouts, The Professor switched to seat 60 next the window that he might lean through and embrace Ethel for another five minutes. He'd barely made contact when a disgruntled R.A.N. man, who'd evidently lost his girl to a Yank earlier in the day, entered the compartment, glowered at his ticket and The Professor, and tapping the latter on the shoulder muttered, "Yu' got me seat." Without stopping for breath The Professor switched to seat 64, which was also next the window, and took up where he'd left off with Ethel (or Beryl).

There was some commotion and swearing at the car door as half a dozen drunks, watching the last few moments of a precious furlough slip away, helped each other aboard. The engineer blew his whistle; made a couple of false starts that nicely settled the baggage, the passengers, and several weak stomachs; and then, slowly, very slowly, the second division of the "mile trine" got under way. Beryl (or Ethel) left us as a "No Clearance" post intervened and all but took off The Professor's head and olive-brown scarf.

Compartment 8 was a long way ahead of the second-class compartments I'd known when traveling with troops, and I said as much. A loquacious Digger on the other side of The Professor heartily agreed with me, and went on to explain that the trains used for troops were of an older, much older, vintage, actually considered in these modern times as third class. I heartily agreed with *him* on that and thought briefly of the genius of a man named George Pullman.

In addition to the Digger and the R.A.N. chap who had insisted The Professor break as we were pulling out, there was a long, thin, sourfaced civilian hunched in seat 64.

The other three seats in No. 8 were empty. We made the most of this, curling up in a variety of uncomfortable positions and sticking our feet in each other's faces in our attempts to sleep. Two or three hours out we stopped and added some new faces, No. 8 getting a baby that cried, a large woman, apparently its mother, and a small, wistful, beaten-looking man, obviously the large woman's husband, and possibly the father of her child. This group put an end to our bawdy stories and, I was afraid, our sleeping. But around 2:00 A.M., after having dropped off to sleep and been thrown to the floor when the engineer tried the ties for a piece, I stretched out on the floor.

48

Between a number of feet, with my overcoat pulled over my face and my head on some sort of steam heater that clanked and growled but gave no heat, I spent a surprisingly restful night. Now and then, of course, somebody tried the door of our compartment by mistake and, discovering his mistake and my face, backed off and slammed the door on my head, but in spite of that I looked healthier than any of the other occupants come dawn. The Professor, in the first weak light, looked particularly unhealthy, so bad in fact, that I overheard the large woman and the R.A.N. chap discussing the possibilities of pushing his body through the window that there might be more room for the rest of us. I woke The Professor in his own interests, but after staring into his face for some minutes was just about ready to put him back to sleep and side with Mama and the R.A.N.

About 9:00 A.M., thirteen hours on the roadbed behind us, we stopped for breakfast. If the "mile trine" had a diner, it had gone north with the first division. Consequently we of the second division left our compartments en masse and surged onto the platform and into the station through a door marked "Refreshments." The Professor and I, who, in spite of a few weeks soft living, could still be pretty self-reliant in a crisis, fought and clawed our way through the press of seething humanity, stiff-armed a couple of small children, and succeeded in grabbing two places with the "first sitting." Our particular sitting sat seven, four of whom were still in the act of lowering their laps when a beefy waitress steamed up and slapped a bowl of cereal under each of our noses.

As we finished this cereal our waitress reappeared and, with a motion like that of a striking cobra, snatched the empty bowls from under our chins, replacing them with some rather nondescript servings of sausages and chips and some very nondescript coffee. These too, ere we had fully closed our mouths on the last bite, were snatched from us; and, had we not gathered by then that no reflective chewing of toothpicks would be tolerated and left hurriedly of our own volition, there is little doubt but that our chairs would likewise have been snatched from under us that the "second sitting" might lose no time in seating themselves and stabbing at their food as it was whisked by.

The "second sitting," while we were eating, either hung over the rail, licking their lips and pawing the ground like cattle watching a block of salt, or lined the refreshment counter and pushed and shoved and fought with the "third sitting" for sandwiches and fruit, thus adding little to what was scarcely a quiet, unhurried meal in the first place. All this snatching and grabbing of plates and swallowing of hot soup, however, was necessary if the second division was to maintain anything approaching a schedule; and, to give credit where credit is due, during the three sittings that I had the opportunity of watching or eating, I saw but one accident. That, after all, may have been no accident, as I suspect the tech-sergeant we later found in the Gent's Lavatory, combing spaghetti and meatballs out of his blond locks, deliberately pinched the waitress' calf.

This incident occurred during lunch, at a place called Casino. The Professor and I were fouled that stop, early in the general surge to the platform. Confused by it all, we lunged from the wrong side of the train, suffering a nasty fall to the cinders. By the time we'd picked ourselves up and dusted the local freight yards off our knees and elbows, the "first sitting" were halfway through their entree, the "second sitting" were on their marks, and the "third sitting" presented a solid phalanx of olive drab, calico, and blue serge backsides

51

that The Professor and I, in our weakened condition, knew we could never penetrate. Nor did we manage sandwiches and tea at the counter but were, instead, forced to deal with a couple of the twelve-year-old racketeers who infested the station's dirtier corners, their sharp, shrewd little eyes peeled for American servicemen traveling second class and too discouraged to fathom the sittings system. In exchange for the greater share of that day's "MALR" two of them

supplied us with cold meat pies and warm sarsaparilla. In all, the inauspicious beginning of an afternoon that went from there to something worse.

The A.M. had been, comparatively speaking, pleasant enough. The R.A.N., finding an acquaintance, a WAAAF posted to Towns-ville, in a near-by compartment, had left No. 8 and inflicted his presence on this acquaintance and the other occupants of No. 6 until eleven. Returning he'd been in much better spirits than the night before and had even condescended to chortle at a couple of bawdy stories The Professor managed to rasp his way through while the large woman and her children were off to the Winston Churchill (W.C.). I'd dozed some myself, read bits of a pretty low-powered, six-penny sex magazine I'd found under the seat, and read and reread my orders for the thrill they gave me. Even Lemon Face thawed to the point of cracking a toothy grin when a particularly nasty jolt seemed to snap The Professor's spinal cord.

The afternoon, however, was something else. In the first place, our train, which consisted of eight passenger carriages and, at the rear, a baggage car, was half full of camp-bound American soldiers. Furloughees, returning after seven days in the bes' damn city or points south, by far the greater share of them were much too intent on squeezing all the so-called enjoyment possible out of that half of their "two days travel time" they were then experiencing. Theoretically they occupied the first four carriages. Now what our baggage car contained I don't know, but from the persistent way in which the occupants of the first four carriages insisted on hacking and pushing their way through the last four—of which ours was the first —I would have guessed along about 2:00 P.M. that nothing less than Earl Carroll's Vanities, neatly wrapped and labeled, could account for the stampede.

In addition to the drunks clogging the narrow passage on their way to or from the baggage car, a considerable number of passengers, who had somehow slipped aboard during our luncheon stop, stood or leaned or slouched or sat (if they owned luggage that would bear sitting on) around in the aisles.

Presuming the age of chivalry to be not yet quite dead, I'd given my seat to an unnecessary old lady who'd gotten aboard a few miles north of our luncheon stop, thinking, in my innocence, that when my knees buckled I would go and slump in the doorway of No. 8, and the old lady would offer me my seat back, and somebody else would in turn give her his. The age of chivalry died with me that afternoon. I slumped in the doorway of No. 8 regularly, from 2:30 on but the old lady made no offers of any kind, nor did anyone else show the slightest indication of leaving their seat for anything less than the end of the world. Thus I got the full benefit of the crowded

conditions so rampant in the steerage and of the drunks who had evidently mistaken it for the Lincoln Memorial Highway.

Our train, I'll swear, missed not one siding during the entire trip. Every hour on the hour we switched on to one and stopped. And waited. For no apparent reason. This became increasingly disgusting as the afternoon wore on and I wore out. Word eventually came back to us (whispered from ear to ear through the first four cars, I guessed) that these stops were made that the "southbound mile trine" might have the right-of-way. The exact whereabouts of this southbound was evidently unknown to all concerned, for though we waited time and again, it refused to come out of its tunnel until we'd been some twenty-two hours out. When it did go roaring by it was greeted with a cracked, wavering cheer from us of the second division, northbound, who could still speak.

We got under way ourselves then, and rolled for perhaps three-quarters of a mile, attaining a speed of at least fifteen miles an hour, when another shout went up from the rear of the train. Poking our heads through the windows disclosed that two of the drunks who had been getting off at all the sidings and annoying any girls unlucky enough to be passing by had delayed too long in regaining the train, and were now manfully attempting a staggering gallop intended to catch us. Neither did, though they chased us for almost a mile.

I've often wondered what happened to those two soldiers. Did they catch a passing freight, or did they settle down in the hills, marry, and raise goats? Or might they be beating their way north, tie by tie, with a charge of desertion staring them in the face? I don't know. But knowing the American Army, I'd guess they flagged a passing freight and rode the engine to their destination, arriving late on the day of grace that is added to furlough travel time and meanwhile winning two drivewheels off the engineer shooting crap.

Twenty-four hours to the minute, it was, when we at last rolled into our destination. How far behind schedule that left us, I don't know. Nor did any one else, I suspect. The closest any of the railroad employees had attempted when we asked them, "When will we get there?" was "Tomorrer afternoon sometime." At any rate that part of our journey masquerading on our orders as "Govt rail T" was over, and that was enough for us. The Professor and I bundled our luggage out of No. 8 and onto the platform, where a blaring public address system greeted us with: "All American Personnel—report to your R.T.O., to the left of the ticket barrier. All American personnel—report to your R.T.O., to the left of the ticket barrier. All American personnel—. . ." It was late and the station was but dimly lit and we were tired and nobody was expecting us anyway. The Professor and I did not report to our R.T.O. to the left of the ticket barrier. Instead, eluding a couple of sleepy MP's, we slipped through the barrier in the darkness, fled down the ramp,

caught a tram (the city was familiar to me) to the open arms of our old friends, the American Red Cross Service Club, got beds, had doughnuts and coffee, and went to sleep.

Now as a dyed-in-the-dust, working infantryman, with my ankles dragging in the gravel, I hated the Air Corps. Them and their silver wings and leather jackets and advertisements and glamor. I hated them and I said so, and now I'd like to retract a few of the things I said. The Air Corps are okay. They have their share of Chairborne Commandos, perhaps, but the working Air Corps, as an arm of the service, probably spends more time closer to the war than does any other, while their ordinary day's business—flying—obviously involves more risk, if less effort, than does hiking. For that I'll give them credit. I'll give them more for just being great guys, a little contemptuous of S.O.P. and Army ways in some instances, but with a wonderful knack of getting things done and going through the channels afterwards. All right, so the Air Corps is a great thing. I can't truthfully say that I feel the same of D.A.T., the Directorate of Air Transport.

Having concluded my "Govt rail T" still some hundreds of miles short of the first A.P.O. listed on my orders, I turned to D.A.T. who would, as my orders had it, slap me aboard the "first available MOCA" ("military or commercial aircraft"). Actually, "first available MOCA" merely suggests that the EM concerned will be spared the discomfort of Govt rail, motor, or water T, and will, instead, lose several days all in one place, waiting for a plane, a priority, or the weather.

Taking a long view of the situation, the necessity for sweating it out could be blamed on our failure to listen to General Billy Mitchell some years ago or to listen to anybody who said it could happen to us some years later. Now and then an exceptionally far-sighted soldier will blame the known shortage of duraluminum and synthetic rubber. The rest of us look no further than the D.A.T. office that is telling us "You'll jes' have t' sweat it out" (the quick brush). I favor this view myself.

A few days later the photographer, whose name was Richard, ar-

rived, and he and I stormed D.A.T. A sulking sergeant said, "Lemme see ya' orders," glanced at them and confirmed our worst suspicions: our priority was such that barring the day our planned production of 100,000 planes a year was delivered intact to the Southwest Pacific, we would sweat it out. "You ain't got no priority there," he told us. Thus began our battle with the priority system, now entering its seventeenth month.

Courtesy Yank *Magazine*

All MOCA travel is, supposedly, on a strict priority basis. This may not be news exactly. You've no doubt read, now and again (I've run into it half a dozen times), a pleasant little tale to the effect that a private, traveling on government business, can bump a brigadier general, traveling for pleasure, out of the No. 3 bucket seat on a C-47 without anybody batting an eye. Believe me, it seldom happens. In the first place, few BG's travel for pleasure; in the second place . . . well, it seldom happens.

But to get back to the priorities. These run from triple-A (appearing as AAA on damn few travel orders) through double-A-one (AA1), double-A-two (AA2) and so on down to single-A-two, a

priority that means the would-be tourist is simply moving from his present station to the D.A.T. waiting list for an indefinite period. There is a firm belief among many EM that the whole system was primarily designed to facilitate the movement of commissions from forward areas to protracted leaves in the larger cities. This is probably not altogether true. As a second lieutenant T.C. (Transportation Corps) once explained to me, in the early days of the Pacific war there was no such thing as a priority. The EM or O concerned simply went to the strip, cornered the pilot of one of the few available aircraft of any kind, asked him which way he was going, and got aboard.

As the war progressed, however, and more personnel arrived, all desiring MOCA, seats became harder to get. Then one day a clever A.G. (Adjutant General) writing a travel order for a friend, added the magic symbol: "A1" priority. Within a week another A.G. (another smoothie) bestowed on a friend an "A" Priority. Close behind came other smoothies, with double-A-ones and double-A's and triple-A-ones. Before the "A" keys on thousands of typewriters became hammered out of shape, a central controlling agency was hurriedly established, a limited number of triple-A's (for emergency use only) was locked away in a place known only to a few, and D.A.T., with the help of G.H.Q. Regulating Officers, devised, mimeographed, revised, and remimeographed a number of forms intended to bring order out of the chaos at the strips. Or so, at least, my second lieutenant T.C. guessed. I am inclined to believe him.

I know, at least, that on strips but recently captured from the Japanese, the procedure is simply "Ast the pilot." ("Which way ya' goin', Lieutenant?" "Silly Silly, I think." "Got room f' a pas-

senger?" "Yeah, sure, get in.") On strips not so recently captured from the Japanese, a tired soldier ensconced in a dusty grass shack, behind a *New York Times* dated April 29th, 1941, may ask languidly for one or more of the four things a soldier has instead of a birthright—name, rank, serial number, and organization.

Retreating yet another hundred miles or so, to a strip we built ourselves on once (briefly) held Jap territory, it is generally necessary to produce some kind of orders. From Moresby south (and north, too, for a long ways by this time) orders are not only produced but a copy handed over to D.A.T., who in return hand the applicant three to five copies—depending on whim, as near as I could ever figure out—of a form on which he may write his own name, rank, serial number, organization, weight, baggage weight, total weight, present station, station to which transportation is desired, basis for request, phone number, and signature. Thus we advance.

And thus, during the spring and summer of 1943, the whole brief history of air transportation could be seen in the making, in the course of eight hours flying time or less.

Richard, however, as we slunk out of the Transportation Office following our first encounter with D.A.T., saw little hope of our ever flying anywhere, even for a quick trip around the city. We need not have worried; before the day was over half a dozen acquaintances had scoffed at our fears, saying loftily, "Hell, I'll get you a ride. Go see . . ." (and they named a variety of sergeants, lieutenants, and captains, all Air Corps, who would, so they said, fix us up at the drop of a hat).

For three days we tracked these men to their lairs in various downtown office buildings, running the gamut from Statistical Control Office, Rear Echelon, Fifth Air Force Headquarters, to Air Freight Control Office, Queensland L. of C. Area. To a man, and to an O, these gentlemen were brokenhearted over their inability to furnish us with anything less than a Fortress, as of that instant. In some cases they told us, "Jeez, Mac, we just ain't got anything going"; in other cases their planes were all up north; still others told us, "Hell, I'd like to, but G.H.Q. is checking up now. It'd be worth my stripes to pull a fast one." Several sergeants blamed the way their hands were tied on "this new major, he's a sonuvabitch."

Richard and I didn't know it at the time, but every member of the A.U.S. overseas who has so much as shaken hands with a pair of silver wings apparently labors under the delusion that that entitles him to promise MOCA to every other member of the A.U.S. he subsequently meets. And "Hell, Mac, I can get you a ride," with Richard and me, is about as popular as that other expression, "Well, boys, home by Christmas."

At this point we got a couple of frantic wires from the home office urging we get the hell out of town. There was a "show" coming off up north. Remembering, in desperation, the advice of the tech-sergeant at the Red Cross, we tried Operations—or "Ops," in Air Corps parlance—at the —1st Air Depot. Located in one corner of a hangar crouched on the far side of several square miles of airfield situated on the outskirts of town, Ops was presided over, as near as we could discern, by a to begin with none too friendly corporal. We inquired about a ride. During the ensuing conversation it came out that the corporal and Richard hailed from the same state, Massachusetts, and had both whiled away some carefree civilian hours in the same roadhouses. Well, hell. That, in these times, is sufficient basis for a warm and enduring friendship. The corporal thawed visibly. "You got orders?" he asked. We produced our orders. Scarcely glancing at them, the corporal said, "You be out here at five o'clock tomorrer morning. We'll fix you up."

At eight-thirty the following morning Richard and I boarded our first "first available MOCA." The protocol involved—and this, I think, was where my love for the Air Corps began—was insignificant. Stumbling into Ops at 5:00 A.M., bleary with sleep but hopeful, we approached the corporal who, wonder of wonders, remembered us. Calling to a downy-faced young man with tarnished first lieutenant's bars on his shoulders, he said, "I got two more passengers here, Lieutenant. You got room?" The young man, who looked as if he

had had a rather harrowing evening, said, "Yeah, I guess so," dug a
crumpled piece of paper—the "manifest"—out of his jacket pocket,
smoothed it against the wall, and with a stub of indelible pencil that
he kept wetting with his tongue wrote our last names and serial
numbers on it. Then he told us, "Just keep an eye on me," and returned to discussing with three other pilots, in detail, punctuated
with coarse laughter, the highlights of his harrowing evening. Lest
we be left behind, Richard and I, between us, kept four eyes on our
pilot until well after eight-thirty. By that time we were flying at
2000 feet.

With several bored Air Corps men aboard, cursing the one who
had condemned them to a "47" while there were two "24's" on the
field, I could scarcely admit any thrill I might have felt but tried,
instead, to appear as blasé as they. Actually, this wasn't too difficult.
Douglas C-47's, in the eyes of the Air Corps in the Southwest Pa-

cific, are generally considered to be about as glamorous as a beer truck and riding one about as breath-taking as hitching a lift on a beer truck used to be.

So I sat calmly enough, with my feet on a pile of barracks bags and two wooden boxes marked: "Sig Supply 0 925 TO 5 AACS Horn Island RUSH," and bummed matches and talked shop with a Pfc. from an ack-ack outfit who was sitting on my right. Shop, in our case, being: Were ya' down on furlough? Ain't Brisbane a hole? How long ya' been over? (Things have sure changed since then, huh?) Good officers and bad officers. Them bastards in the States. How many times ya' had malaria? What outfit ya' from? Ain't Guinea a sonavubitch? How long ya' think the war'll last? Where ya' think we're going next (speaking of MacArthur's combined forces)? How ya' stand on goin' home? Our last affairs (she was engaged, but it didn't make no difference). Where ya' from in the States? Ain't Rocky a sonavubitch?

Now C-47's were designed essentially for freight, and personnel often understandably feel that they are aboard at all only through the tolerance of a number of auxiliary gas tanks. I have always felt too that the crew of a 47 looked on personnel as something of considerably less value than gas tanks, something that was being shuttled from one point to another simply because there weren't any gas tanks available. I can see their point; gas tanks invariably get a much higher priority. Personally, I've since been off-loaded at some pretty godforsaken spots in favor of engine parts or a damaged nose wheel.

Designed as it is for freight, a 47 lacks most of the accouterments that make civilian air travel such a pleasure—stewardesses, for one thing. The seats, which unfold from beneath the windows, are scarcely conducive to comfort either, being constructed of but reasonably soft aluminum or, more recently, some kind of plastic. At 7000 feet a noticeable chill is apparent. Perhaps the best means of passing the time is by sleeping, but with a full load—say twenty men and their baggage—aboard, not more than four or five of the more initiative will find room to sprawl. Should the trip be "rough," sleeping isn't too practicable either. Reading is popular, and a last week's *Guinea Gold* (Port Moresby's daily) or a last month's *Yank* (Down-Under edition) or a last year's *Reader's Digest* generally go the rounds of the passengers who aren't sleeping or too engrossed in conversation. A few Pocket Books, mostly mysteries, are usually in

evidence. Street & Smith appears to run a poor fifth. This is merely a personal Daniel-Starch Survey, however, and need not be accepted as too reliable.

I'd worked my way through two corpses in *The Closed Cart Door Murders* and given it back to the owner, or rather, the staff sergeant who had stolen it from the Red Cross Club, and was amusing myself with a four-months-old copy of *Newsweek*. Knowing full well from an earlier perusal of the remnants of a month-old St. Louis *Post-Dispatch* whether or not "The Periscope" had guessed right as to "what was to be expected in tomorrow's news," it was rather an amusing pastime, until one of the crew stuck his head out of the door marked "Crew Only" and grunted, "Everybody move forward." We landed a few moments later.

The copilot, as he scrambled over our luggage on his way to the door, informed us: "We'll be here 'bout twenty minutes." Richard and I crawled out to stretch our legs with the other passengers and, following two air gunners who seemed to know what they were doing, presently wound up on the other side of the sun-flooded field, behind the hangars and a drab brown D.A.T. office, in an Australian Salvation Army hut, where we had tea and cookies, for free. Richard and I, who still suffered from a fear of being left behind, were back at the plane in well under twenty minutes but found no sign of the pilot, copilot, crew chief, or radioman. Half an hour passed before the crew chief showed up to get a jacket and two cans of pineapple out of the tail compartment. We asked him what was holding us up. He muttered briefly, "We're sweatin' out the weather," and took off in the direction of the Ops shack, leaving us to our own devices. Thus it was that we were introduced to that great hold-me-back of travel by air in the Southwest Pacific—"the weather."

It was well after 2:00 P.M. when, "the weather" having evidently improved and the crew having returned from downtown with their bellies full of steak (I add this merely as a statement of fact, no innuendo intended), we took off again. Our own field had been bathed in brilliant sunshine at all times and I, frankly, was a little skeptical about "the weather." All I knew was what I'd overheard the chief telling the radioman—"They's a front movin' down. If it goes inland we'll probably R.O.N." (remain overnight). The radioman had replied, "In Tville maybe? I know a girl there."

Presently we loaded and I waded through two more corpses in *The Closed Cart Door Murders.* I gave them up (still unsolved) as we started down again and had my nose pressed flat against the window when we broke through the clouds over mile on mile of bush and what, from where I was sitting, looked like some kind of sprawling W.P.A. project. As we circled lower I gathered that the project was really an airstrip, three or four airstrips, in fact, all criss-crossing each other and all literally hacked out of the bush. The crew chief stuck his head out of the cockpit door and told us all to move forward again. Up to this point I'd been religiously obeying a stenciled sign: "No Smoking During Landings or Take-off," but seeing three or four of the Air Corps present all puffing away un-

perturbed, I brazenly clung to my own butt while we landed. I was fast becoming an old Air Corps man myself.

As we climbed out of the plane I gathered from the conversation between the crew chief and the radioman that wherever we were it certainly wasn't Tville (Tville, according to the chief, having "closed in") and that the radioman not only knew no girls in the vicinity but considered it extremely unlikely that there even were any girls. I agreed with him.

The field at which we'd stopped had, perhaps in the days of the Coral Sea Battle, been an up and coming fighter base literally ahum with the industry of war; but now, the "other side of the Hump" (or Owen Stanleys) safely ours, its days of death and glory were over. Except for odd flights of fighters that stopped to refuel on their way to the islands, it was deserted. And nothing appears quite so desolate and forlorn and deserted as a military installation that's been left behind the war. This particular installation, stuck as it was in the middle of the bush and evidently several hundred miles from nowhere, had probably been forlorn enough at the best of times.

71

Our plane had taxied to a stop not more than a mile and a quarter from the Operations shack (Richard and I were to learn that this is S.O.P.), the crew had climbed out and with their baggage piled into a dusty jeep that had come roaring out to meet us, and promptly roared away. This, too, we've learned, is S.O.P. Left alone, we passengers presently caught a ride on a battered old truck of evident Italian vintage, full of dusty R.A.A.F. ground personnel clad mostly in shorts and burnt the deep red color of the surrounding landscape.

Over in the Operations shack a jaded staff sergeant (A.A.F.) looked at us listlessly and gave up his wan attempts at driving away the cloud of flies that hovered over his head long enough to inform

us that the American personnel in the vicinity consisted of a detachment of the —5th Service Squadron located at the far end of No. 2 strip and a station hospital located "in town," which was about fifteen miles away.

We remarked that there didn't appear to be much going on around the field. The sergeant said, "Hell, there ain't even a war. All I do is sit." He went on to explain that he belonged to a weather detachment, exiled to this bunghole of creation five months earlier and, he suspected, since forgotten by the powers that controlled their destiny. He called down bitter curses on a friend who had spent a similar length of time in a weather control station in Brisb'n (he referred to this friend as a "fat cat"); and described in horrid detail the kind of food he'd been forced to swallow while messing with a local R.A.A.F. squadron, before the arrival of the U.S. service detachment.

A lieutenant offered us a ride in his jeep. While we bounced the fifteen miles to town through the thick red haze the slanting afternoon sun made of the dusty atmosphere, he told us that he was the C.O. of the weather detachment exiled to this bunghole of creation five months earlier and since, he was sure, forgotten by the powers that controlled their destiny; heartily blasphemed a friend (recently promoted to captain) who'd spent the same five months in the Brisb'n weather control station (he described the supposed life this friend was leading with a single sneering word—"Hardships!"); and told us with no regard for international relations about the alleged chow he'd been forced to eat while subsisting with the officer's mess of the local R.A.A.F. squadron . . .

Next morning, other people getting up woke me at 4:00 A.M. Half an hour later, Richard and I and the rest of the passengers and crews straggled into the mess hall where a fat jolly captain, A.C. (assisted by two morose second cooks who were cursing the fate that had forced us to R.O.N. with them) was dishing out eggs and cereal and coffee. Richard and I ate heartily though we were still half asleep. The Air Corps present, on the other hand, who, from months of doing it, could apparently crawl out of bed at 4:00 A.M. and step into a chill foggy morning and still remain human, were all very boisterous and profane. Until a pilot who'd landed late the previous evening came in, got his eggs, sat down, and said perfunctorily, more or less as one might mention last night's bridge to a wife sitting on the other side of a newspaper, "Well, Smitty got it yesterday. . . ."

There was a sudden quiet. Somebody said, "Yeah?"

The pilot nodded. "West of Cloncurry," he said. "Must've been lost or something. Compass out maybe. Tried to bring her down anyway. Got a wing into the ground or a hill or something. Burned. Only ten minutes out of Clon, too. . . ."

Somebody said, "Jesus," almost reverently.

The cold and dirty breath of war was suddenly close to us.

Somebody said, "What was he flyin'?"

The pilot said, "FS [aircraft call letters] Personnel."

A passenger asked, "Anybody . . . . ?"

The pilot shook his head. "To a crisp," he said.

Somebody said, "Sonavubitch"; somebody else, "Now they'll start talkin' chutes again."

Richard and I went back to our cereal, but those of the crews and pilots who had known Smitty talked on—of his good points, of the great guy he'd been, of the damn fine flyer he'd been, of the good times they'd had with him in various places in the U.S. and/or Australia. Gradually their conversation shifted to the close ones they'd had themselves . . . of a port engine that conked out high over the Coral Sea, for instance, with an overload of auxiliary gas tanks cramming the cargo compartment . . . of the radioman who'd crawled and squirmed between the tanks, sprung the cargo door and watched it torn off and blown into the elevator surfaces, then braced himself against the slip stream, 7000 feet above the Coral Sea with nothing between him and it but God and air, and one by one manhandled the tanks out into that air . . . their altitude down to 20 feet when the last tank went out, making Cairns flying through, not over, the Great Barrier Reef, fixing the engine and flying on to Townsville that afternoon. . . .

By their own admission every flight crew at that breakfast table had been scared blue on several occasions and had faced, calmly enough, their destiny running out, over deep blue water, jungle, or the Never-Never land of the Northern Territory. But they were still flying, and their close ones, described, as always, profanely, were almost a grim, ironical, do-your-worst-and-to-hell-with-you kind of humor.

Shortly after five we piled aboard a couple of GI trucks and were bounced through the chill and the fog to the field. Shortly after six, our hearing dulled by the continuous roar of two dozen motors as they warmed up, we took off into a slate gray sky. There was another chapter in *The Closed Cart Door Murders* but it failed to keep Smitty off my mind. I sweated out a perfectly routine flight

74

through thin scattered clouds, a perfectly routine descent through the same and a perfectly routine landing. At Townsville.

Townsville. Tville—the crossroads, in '43, of the Southwest Pacific. And by all GI accounts the hottest, dirtiest, lousiest, toughest, most overcrowded troop town this side of Alexandria, Louisiana.

TOWNSVILLE—or Tville as it was more generally known—might be described as the Naples of the Southwest Pacific. The equivalent of the local chamber of commerce claimed that it was, or had been before the war, "the Gateway to the Tropics." I am indebted to "a beat-down Red Cross Girl" (in her own words) for the more apt description, "tarnished Gateway to the Tropics." It was generally agreed that Americans were largely responsible for the tarnish. As a veteran of two years in the Gateway told me, "it's just that there been so damn many Yanks here for so damn long the town has plain give up."

The peacetime population of Tville had been approximately 35,000; its wartime strength neared 160,000 civilians, plus a gigantic sprawling kind of U.S. Army overseas base including an air field that handles much freight and many planes and personnel, a base section that handles a great bulk of the theater's incoming supplies and troops, a huge ordnance dump of salvageable vehicles, small ships and A.T.C. personnel and installations, amphibian engineers and several L.C.M.'s that had somehow been left behind by their unit and were making the most of it until orders caught up with them, and merchant shipping lying at anchor.

C-47's of the Troop Carrier Command roared overhead regularly, heading out over the bay for the Islands or coming in low from points north, points south, and the endless miles of nothingness that stretched west to Cloncurry and across the Northern Territory to Darwin. 24's, a few 17's, A20's, 25's, 26's and fighters till hell wouldn't have them and a limited number of aged Australian Airways De Havilands filled the rest of the sky. Now and then the multimotored, cigar-shaped silhouette of an A.T.C. (Air Transport Command) C-54 came in high over the bay.

Tville's rail service was unique; trains that were due Tuesday arrived regularly on Wednesday and everybody took it for granted.

There was no war in Tville. The vicinity had been raided once, a hit-and-run affair in early 1942, that resulted in the loss of several cubic yards of mud flat, but that was the extent of its active participation. During the forty-eight hours of the Coral Sea Battle of course—as the inhabitants who had not evacuated were wont to tell us—a couple of zealous beaver ack-ack crews had banged away at gulls. Air-raid wardens had been called out and the VDC (Volunteer Defence Corps) armed with pistols and shot guns collected from the local sportsmen had been alerted.

But those days were long past and almost forgotten, as were most of any thanks possibly due the Americans who, flying 25's, 26's, and the remains of a few Forts, had "saved" Tville. The native sons who had been burying their family silver at the time hadn't forgotten and never would, but the remainder of the 160,000 odd civilians knew Americans mostly as people who bought everything in sight and then complained loudly because there wasn't more. And the Americans then in Tville were inclined to take Tville at its face value, and curse it and all it stood for, bitterly and repeatedly. Not that this particularly worried the inhabitants, either permanent or transient. They'd survived it too long. They were inured to it and to Americans. They had just plain give up.

There was a backwash of war in Tville. Troops, mostly Air

77

Corps, were constantly passing through, lying over to sweat out the weather or their priority or a new ship. They gave the town a kind of cosmopolitan, tourist-camp flavor. And there is something about combat and combat areas that isn't shaken off in a matter of hours. The soldiers passing through had lent Tville a sordid kind of glamor.

It had the state of mind of a boom town that couldn't stand the pace. The troops in Tville, exclusive of the early arrivals who had married locally, settled down, and were already listening, enrapt, to the first garbled words of little Australian-Americans, had the boom-town, to-hell-with-it, grab-it-while-you-can philosophy. The civilian population was beyond caring.

But I, personally, shall never forget Tville, nor will anybody else I think who was stationed there. For transients Tville was undoubtedly the second layer of hell, but for those who were stationed there more or less permanently it provided some weird and varied experiences.

The Professor having come by boat, had arrived before me. So I got off my first 47, registered with a sergeant of MP's in the control station, and phoned The Professor from the near-by Red Cross canteen. It took me some time to reach him. Yes indeed. The Tville telephone system probably deserves several hundred thousand words, many of them profane. The American Army had immediately snapped up all the experienced telephone operators. The civilian exchange had perforce fallen back on, I was inclined to believe,

fourteen-year-old girls with speech impediments. Consequently the procedure and result of slamming a call through a civilian and two Army exchanges beggars description. I once watched a T-5 try it for an hour and forty minutes and wind up with two utter strangers who were discussing a grave site screaming at him because they thought he was the operator.

It was some time before I heard The Professor's familiar rasp on the other end of the line. He said he "didn't have any transportation," a familiar phrase, and suggested I bum a ride or catch an Army bus into town. I thumbed a ride with two R.A.A.F. wing commanders, found The Professor slouched outside the particular U.S. Army office where he had had a desk allotted him. He suggested we go over to his hotel and get me a bed. (We were on $5 per day per diem at the time, a fact that made it a little difficult to respect anything less than a major.) Because it was Sunday the front door of The Professor's hotel was locked, and we went around through the alley to the back, brushing aside a dirty little boy who told us, "Yer can't get in, Yank, the beer's off." It apparently seldom occurred to any of the natives that two Yanks might be scouting around a hotel for something besides beer.

Inside we dug the proprietress out of her copy of *Truth* and, thanks to The Professor's way with landladies, she presently agreed to give me a bed on the porch at three bob the night. The Professor had a bona fide room, less any facilities for washing, but it had taken him two weeks of plying the landlady and chambermaids with chocolate bars to get it, and it was not to be expected that I could get a room without a similar campaign.

In all I spent several weeks at The Queensland. Now and then, to be sure, coming home late, I found my bed already occupied by another Yank. Our landlady was a little "forgetful." On these occasions I slept in any other bed that was vacant, or if there weren't any vacant, I failed to sleep on a retired studio couch that decorated the back porch.

Once or twice when The Professor was out of town I slept in his bed, disturbed only—and then considerably—by Pearl the Chambermaid.

Our hotel featured a battered sink on the back porch that was more or less suitable for shaving and minor wash jobs. When it came to showers we relied on the local Red Cross.

As a matter of fact, I am deeply indebted to the Red Cross for a number of the things I got—and that happened to me—in Tville. And it was in Tville that I met my first Red Cross girl. Prior to that a Red Cross girl had simply been a female surrounded by thirty soldiers. In Tville, thanks to The Professor's having wormed his way into their confidence, I met some Red Cross girls. Backstage, you might say.

Well, they were Americans; we talked the same language. They'd joined up in the first place for a variety of reasons, but mostly because they simply wanted to be *in it*. Joining, most of them had been a little "hepped up." Possibly they had even imagined themselves binding up a few wounds. Well, the only wounds they'd bound up were the skinned knuckles and black eyes suffered by soldiers who got in fights. They'd come prepared to pitch in and spare nothing. They were typically American and their reactions to the somewhat lackadaisical efforts of a great share of the civilian help they encountered were likewise typical—near horror. They felt that they were doing only a fraction of the good they might do, and talked endlessly, and very bitterly, of the way they were stuck in Tville doing so little for so few when they might have been in the islands doing so much, they imagined, for so many.

They referred to their service club as the "Roseland," referred to themselves as "taxi dancers," and called the newly arrived staff assistants who were still gurgling with an urge to dispense good works "eager beavers." They dragged themselves off to the service club ten or twelve or fourteen hours a day all the same, danced their feet off as far up as the ankles, took more than any girl probably should from a lot of GI's who weren't entirely to blame however, constantly bewailed the club improvements they so desperately wanted to institute but couldn't, dragged themselves back to their billets, said "Oh God! Tomorrow night I've got to get some sleep," and sat up and talked shop far into the night.

They were never off duty. They were "beat down." But every once in a while, talking—downright talking, straight and honest—to a GI who wasn't being average at the time, only himself, their faith

in humanity and themselves and what they were trying to do was temporarily propped up and their spirits soared, temporarily, like a climbing 38. Sometimes they cried about it. And—and this should serve as some kind of a conclusion—the thought of quitting never entered their minds.

I know that without any Red Cross at all, without a Red Cross cafeteria to eat in on Sundays when 99% of the native restaurateurs close up and go fishing, without any Red Cross canteens where we loaf while sweating out a plane, and without any service clubs at all (service clubs where we write letters on Red Cross stationery or bum a pack of Red Cross cigarettes or steal a book from the club library or perhaps just sit and talk of what the Red Cross isn't doing

"Why did I join the Red Cross? Well, once and for all,
Mac, it was like this: I'd been giving my blood, see, pint
by pint, and when they had it all, I came over after it."
(Courtesy Yank *Magazine)*

for us) without any of these things it would be a decidedly more
miserable war than it is. They can have my dollar.

I learned a lot of things in Tville via other agencies than the
American Red Cross. Faced as it was with many times its normal
population, the essentials in Tville were hard enough come by, while
the luxuries should have been impossible. That we enjoyed a number of good times anyway says a great deal for the enterprising
spirit of Americans anywhere. The Professor from the moment he'd
hit town had made friends with a number of gentlemen, both A.U.S.
and Australian born, who controlled the more desirable commodities
from chickens, fried or on the wing, through various brands of
liquor, to theater tickets and Stateside N.B.C. biscuits. The Profes-

sor referred to all these people as "connections." The best connection by far was a sergeant of MP's, who was himself known as "Connections."

Connections (I am speaking of the sergeant now) in civilian life had worked variously at pro football, prize fighting, gumshoeing,

bodyguarding, and for a number of years the night-club racket. We owed a great deal of our success to Connections, who generally had at his disposal the Tville version of a station wagon—a 2½-ton truck.

Now and then, through the efforts of a young sergeant named Jack, we wound up with a trip ticket that read: "Basis for request— organized recreation." This allowed that we might more or less legally transport females in Connections' 2½ ton. Technically we were probably open to court martial on a number of counts, but there is a kind of unwritten code among MP's (as between civilian gumshoes who seldom arrest a plumbered brother member of the force) that assured us of at least a ten minute start so long as Connections was driving.

Without the accomplishments of another lad named Moonlight, we wouldn't have been nearly the gay young set that we were either. Moonlight, who worked in the A.P.O. because in civilian life he'd repossessed automobiles, following a lengthy campaign, had managed to attain a certain standing in the eyes of a domestically estranged and not exactly young WENL named "Fluffy."

Fluffy had a house. Since I was looked upon as a fat sleazy capitalist because I had, sometimes, a bed on the porch at The Queensland instead of one-sixth of a pyramidal tent pitched half a mile out of town in the middle of the local dog track, you can imagine the position occupied by anybody who had a house in Tville. Of necessity Moonlight had to keep Fluffy in cigarettes, matches, and Aqua-Velva (which she apparently drank, from the way it disappeared); but the use of a house was well worth this investment.

No doubt about it, the combined talents of Connections, Moonlight, and Jack gave us a long start on the masses. But a straightforward account of a typical safari would perhaps leave a clearer impression of the situation. For instance, there was a particular Tuesday. . . .

The Professor and I were seated at his desk in the base special-service office when Connections walked in, described briefly his wantonness of the evening before, and said quietly, "There's a new Liberty in." The Professor, much to his regret, was standing in line for lunch with a young lady from the C.E.B. (Civilian Employment Bureau, U.S. Army) that noon, but I was free, so about eleven o'clock Connections and I got aboard his motorcycle and splashed down to the jetty.

Connections' prestige got us by the guard post. Connections visited the jetty regularly, in line of duty and for the more personal purpose of becoming acquainted with the chief stewards of Liberty ships as fast as they docked; besides he knew all the guards.

We found the new Liberty—the George W. Something it was—breezed by the MP on guard on the gangplank, Connections favoring him with a "H'ya, Jake," and found the chief steward in his cabin reading a *True Story* magazine. He said his name was Harry and that he hailed from New Orleans. Connections dug into memories of his night-club days and for twenty minutes he and Harry discussed the various clubs that had bounded Bourbon Street in '39. Connections was wearing his brassard and during the introductions had managed to flash, significantly, his credentials, which consisted of a U.S. Army driver's license, an identity card, a jetty pass, and a long-expired blue card that had once allowed him entrance to the base-section ammunition dump. A pretty imposing collection of documents in all, I think they left Harry, whose conscience was possibly not as clean as his freshly laundered P-jacket, a little nervous. At least, when Connections mentioned that he must in line of duty "inspect the ship," Harry was all cooperation.

So the inspection got underway and led swiftly enough to the storeroom, where Connections and I drooled over the quantities of Stateside food in evidence, until Harry offered us a jar of pickles. Then he invited us to lunch. We ate with the C.P.O.'s devouring a meal that surpassed by hundreds of knots anything Tville had to offer; i.e., chicken soup that was hot, chicken fried Stateside, Stateside mashed potatoes and gravy, Stateside canned peas that looked healthy, bread and butter and jam, apple pie, and Stateside coffee.

Over cigarettes and a second cup of coffee, Connections remarked that the "downtown businessmen" as we preferred to be called, rather than one of a blasphemous variety of "Commandos," were planning a little get together and suggested that Harry might like to attend. Harry said he sure would. "I wonder about a briazawd [bree-i-zawd—girl] though," mused Connections.

I knew my cue: "What about Brenda?" I said. Now Brenda was a waitress whose claim to fame was of a kind that left people facing charges. Connections had a picture of her, taken in a bathing suit, that he showed to Harry. As expected, Harry, who had been nine weeks at sea, indicated that at that moment he would gladly trade us the George W's two forward holds and gun crew for a few short hours with Brenda.

We arranged to meet him at the jetty entrance at 7:00 P.M. And as we were leaving Connections added casually that it might be nice if Harry were accompanied by a few goodies from the ship's stores. ... Harry said, "Sure, like what?" and Connections said: "Well, how about a case of lemons, some chutney sauce, tomato juice, butter, maybe ten pounds of coffee, canned pineapple or peaches, some canned peas or asparagus tips, onions, mushrooms, a side of sirloin, and anything else you can find." Then we left.

During the afternoon the word went out that Moonlight Manor would be the scene of a jolly safari beginning at 1900 hours and the presence of all with suitable commodities in tow would be cordially welcomed. Our little Soviet meshed smoothly into high gear. Jack said he could furnish "wheels" beginning at 2200 hours; George said he figured he could hold his jeep until about 1930 hours. I phoned the A.P.O. and prompted Moonlight while he instilled Fluffy with some pre-safari enthusiasm and thus tied the Manor up beyond the shadow of a doubt. This was a detail really; Fluffy was easily impressed. Marlin, a gregarious Pfc. who was Jack's assistant, breezed through the C.E.B. and a near-by Q.M. office spreading the word,

and phoned the W.A.A.A.F. barracks spreading the same word. At 5:00 P.M., as soon as it was open, he dropped into the cafe where Brenda was ogled by servicemen of six nationalities (Laskars not excepted) and informed her that her presence at the Manor that evening was practically a command performance and that somebody would pick her up right after work.

At the last moment a shortage of beer was discovered, so Marlin breezed off again to the Flinders Street Red Cross and extended a cordial invitation to a couple of the staff assistants who happened to be on duty. Because A.R.C. lovelies are, socially, officers, these staff assistants were entitled to the beer ration granted officers in the base —three bottles twice a week. Marlin reminded them of this fact.

(Enlisted men in the base got their beer in a canteen cup through the PX between designated hours on designated evenings, a system that left something to be desired in the way of mad, mad fun.) You see, being classed as officers, these A.R.C.'s can, in the event of capture (a possibility that is a little hard to imagine) demand the rights and privileges of officers. Anyway, the A.R.C. agreed to come and bring their beer and Marlin assured them that somebody would pick them up at 2300 hours. In all, Marlin got eight definites and four probables.

But he was only a single, though important cog. The Professor likewise got busy. Visiting several PX managers he extracted—in

return for what I can't imagine, as The Professor traded mostly on his personality—promises of another six bottles of beer, a box of salted crackers, a case of Coca-Cola, and a 25-pound block of ice. The coke man and the iceman folded, but we got the beer and crackers and two extra guests in the person of the PX manager who supplied the crackers and his girl of the moment. Jimmy, who had a very reliable ice connection, agreed to contract for that essential and did.

Boozey, an Air Corps tech-sergeant on TD in Tville as a procure-ment officer, a position that made him welcome, turned up with two quart bottles of lemonade and the equivalent, in our eyes, of an en-graved invitation—a jug of "Old Court," a raw brand of local fire water that we called "Old Yurf" thanks to the Dickens-like lettering on the label. The Air Corps was further represented by the pilot and copilot of the "Luger Luggin' Lassie," a B-25. Both friends of Jimmy's, both were first lieutenants, but the Air Corps doesn't stand on formality much, and they were at loose ends sweating out an overhaul job on the "Lassie's" port engine. Besides, the pilot, whose name was Noble, had once seen to it that Jimmy got a most important ride from Moresby south several days sooner than D.A.T. had intended he should. The least that Jimmy could do in return was ask them out to the Manor.

There was one other guest, a staff sergeant named Brady. Brady was on his way north to Milne Bay, but had been "awaiting trans-portation" in Tville for more than a week and, being a sharp opera-tor, was therefore pretty well established. He donated two chickens,

dressed, that he had wheedled out of one of three old ladies who sold thin spring chickens to favored members of the U.S. Forces.

With the rest of the syndicate moving as smoothly and efficiently as ever Al Capone's had, Connections and I turned to the liquor situation. "We ain't seen Bill for quite a while," Connections suggested, so off we went to Bill, who held a controlling interest in a wholesale house and was, with all, a very nice fellow. Bill was busy but not so busy that he couldn't push aside the paltry details of money grubbing and retire downstairs to the spirits room to "wet one eye" and then the other and, pleasantly thawed and heartened by our proffer of a jar of Stateside pickles, presently sold us four assorted bottles at a legal price. Bill was a very nice fellow indeed. Without him we would often have been among those mentioned in Scripture as "Ye that thirst," nor could we have cleared that last hurdle on the way to a fine safari.

And a fine safari it was. True, at one point it looked as if our best-laid plans had gone awry, and badly. George failed to hold his jeep until 1930, and consequently we lost half an hour until Noble pulled a fast shuffle with a WENL dispatcher at the base motor pool and got us a staff car that served to pick up Harry, who was accompanied by a friend whose name we did not catch and a fair share of the groceries Connections had recommended. We deposited Harry

and his friend and the groceries and Marlin and Brady at the Manor and sent the staff car back to the pool with a trip ticket bearing Noble's scrawled signature and the notation: "Destination . . . U.S. Air Depot." Cats are skinned in a variety of ways.

Jimmy spent a highly uncomfortable and messy twenty minutes, too, riding the buddy seat of Connections' motorcycle with a fifty pound slab of ice in his lap. Then three of the briazawds failed to

show. And there was some trouble with Fluffy who, when the first contingent arrived, was accusing Moonlight of double-time-Charlie inclinations and telling him he could damn well take his friends and his party some place else. She was mollified with a quick drink and a glimpse of Harry's Stateside goodies.

Then Jack was twenty minutes late in meeting Connections and me and, when he did arrive, informed us that the "wrong man" had been on duty at the truck pool and consequently his trip ticket didn't authorize "organized recreation" after 2200 hours. This wasn't a crisis really; Connections took the wheel, thus assuring us of a certain leniency should a roving "Scooter" (motorcycle patrol) pick us up, and we proceeded to slide through town collecting what dates we could—two WAAAF's and a R.A.N. that we hijacked away from the Red Cross dance and Brenda and a friend that we enticed from the YMCA Toc-H club. The WAAAF's, the R.A.N., Brenda, and her friend, whose name was Joyce, rode in the back of the truck under some blankets. There was no sense in stretching the loyalty of Connections' MP friends any further than necessary.

Back at the Manor, Connections attached himself to the R.A.N. because he had once been a sea scout and refused to do any more driving after other people's dates, so Jack and I had to run the blockade by ourselves when it came to picking up the A.R.C. dollies and their beer and a broken-down phonograph and six ragged sides of boogie-woogie. This wasn't too risky either, since the A.R.C. dollies had been working and might simply have been catching a ride to their billets (which lay in the other direction, but a point's a point). Anyway, we used the 2½'s black-out lights and slid safely through back streets to the Manor. With our arrival the safari gathered momentum.

Harry and The Professor did steaks to a medium-rare turn, there was iced tomato juice; the green peas were, Fluffy said, "beaut!" Connections gathered lemons, gin, and powdered sugar about him and confined himself to gurgling at intervals, "A real Tom Collins!" Brady and Marlin played the piano and sang things like *Shine on Harvest Moon*, accompanied by one of the WAAAF's who knew neither the tune nor the words. Silverbelle, one of the Red Cross girls, had learned that night of a transfer she had been dreading, so there was presently an aura of a farewell party in one corner. As a matter of fact, most of our safaris, in Tville, had an aura of farewell, a transient, grab-it-while-you-can, bitter-sweet air about them; probably what made them the memories they are.

Noble, around 0130 hours, as he put it "had let his copilot take over the controls" and was frightening me half to death by insisting drunkenly that I come and fly with him in the morning. Harry's friend, who had spent three weeks in Oro Bay, and Jimmy got into an argument over the relative hardships suffered by the boys in New Guinea and the Base Section Commandos in Tville, or else it was over the odd Red Cross girl—nobody was quite sure which—and eventually came to blows. Neither was seriously injured and fifteen minutes later swore undying friendship over the remains of a can of tomato juice. Moonlight and Fluffy had another tiff, which ended in her going into her room and locking the door. Things were beyond her control by that time anyway.

The people next door complained of the noise about 0200 hours

and threatened to call the local constabulary, but the local constabulary, and Connections knew it and told the rest of us, was reduced to paddling around on bicycles after 9:00 P.M. and wouldn't leave the station for anything less than murder if it was more than a mile away, which the Manor was, and uphill to boot. So we laughed in the neighbors' faces. About 0300 hours Harry gave Brenda a ring he had acquired nine years before from a Liverpool Greek. Jack and the odd WAAAF retired to the back porch. The Professor lost an hour trying to pour drinks from an empty bottle. Noble broke a vase. George broke two glasses. Marlin was sick. The phonograph played *Pine Top Smith* through it all. It was a highly successful safari that Tuesday night.

Wednesday night I split a warm bottle of beer with Connections. Thursday I explored the possibilities of a four-ounce can of Kraft cheese a lieutenant (j.g.) had given Silverbelle. Thursday was the King's birthday or something and Tville was closed up tight, so The Professor and I haggled a pineapple out of a shrewd civilian named Gum Chew, found it too green to eat and went to bed at 10 o'clock.

Tville had its ups and downs.

I LEFT TVILLE at 0545 of a cool misty morning in a C-47 named "Linda Ann" and arrived at Seven Mile Drome, Port Moresby, four-and-a-half hours later. Now the social chasm in this theater during the summer of 1943 between soldiers who had been in New Guinea and soldiers who had not was as the Grand Canyon. This rift is probably true of all theaters, but the fact that the Australian mainland, exclusive of Darwin and vicinity, was as safe as a church and as comfortable and jolly as any theater of war can be, while New Guinea and the islands were the worst that any theater could offer in the way of discomfort, boredom, and allied disadvantages, made the gulf just that much wider. In almost every GI conversation the question sooner or later came up: "Yu' been t' Guinea?" An affirmative answer promptly engendered a mutual feeling of respect and sympathy closely akin to that shared by early Christian martyrs facing a command performance with two lions. On the other hand, if one of the conversationalists hadn't been to New Guinea, his standing promptly went down like the '29 stock market. He might be thousands of miles from home, the father of a child he'd never seen, and a highly unwilling member of the armed forces generally, but what could *he* talk about? What horrors of war could *he* relate, he who had seen naught but the fat-cat life of a Mainland Commando? Hardships! Any horrors he might mention were simply laughable and like the prattlings of a child. About the only thing soldiers who hadn't been could do was shut up and buy the next round. This caste system, of course, has now pretty well folded; contempt now is reserved for Stateside Commandos.

When I went to New Guinea, Port Moresby was still our advanced base against the Japanese, all the headquarters in the area were "Advons" (Advanced Echelons) and Japanese air raids were at least a possibility. Thus the soldiers in N.G., when I got there, were all martyrs, and until I found somebody who had been there less time than I had or hadn't been there at all, it behooved me to listen and gasp when engaged in conversation. I was generally told, "Yu' shoulda' been here when it was *really* tough. . . ."

As a matter of fact, for almost a year it had behooved me to use my mouth mostly for gasping. I'd spent that year on the Mainland, listening at pretty regular intervals to the horrors of war in New Guinea as expounded by all the soldiers I ever met who had been there. These tales usually began, "Yeah, I just got down from Guinea. First beer I seen in 'leven months. . . ." And with the look of a man who was living on borrowed time, a man who had been called upon to serve his country above and beyond the call of ordinary martyrdom, a man whose tired eyes had seen too much (or too much Foster's Old Ale), the raconteur launched into a detailed description of the horrors of rain, heat, mud, dirt, bully beef, blood, brutality, boredom, bombs, and sudden death that were, I gathered, the daily lot of a soldier in New Guinea. Had N.G. had a tourist bureau, the things I heard would probably have led to that bureau's mass hara-kiri. In short, the U.S. Forces were unanimous and vociferous in their opinion that New Guinea was the leading and original bunghole of creation. No others need apply. Others will, of course. Some 90 per cent of our Army are equally convinced that their station is the world's worst, including a friend of mine in Altus, Oklahoma.

So it was that I applied for transportation north through D.A.T. and said good-by to all the friends I'd made (and some that I hadn't made) in Tville. D.A.T. came through with transportation in thirty-six hours, which might have been considered a phenomenon had The Professor not known the secretary who typed the priority lists. I attended the last of four or five farewell parties, had bitter coffee and doughnuts in the Red Cross canteen at the field at 0400 and per instructions reported next door to the D.A.T. office with my fifty-five pounds of authorized baggage.

The sun was just breaking over the bay, swallowing the ground mist that swirled across the field. A cross section of the forces engaged in the theater was standing around D.A.T.: army, air corps, two or three sailors, A.I.F. with their gear (the A.I.F. always travel complete with pack, rifle, ground sheet, and billy can, as if prepared to do battle at a moment's notice) and four Red Cross men with considerably in excess of the authorized fifty-five pounds of baggage. There were half a dozen nurses in raincoats wearing gas masks, to the consternation and amusement of several soldiers who had discarded their own gas masks months before when they'd been moved over the Owen Stanleys by air and decided, in the face of the space and weight restrictions that a small still would be of more practical value. A brigadier general and his retinue of scraping lieutenants shared a bench with an MP and his prisoner, an unconcerned young man who was being forcibly returned to his unit following a three-week extension of furlough instituted by himself and without proper authority. A war correspondent was, trying to cram a half-empty bottle of whiskey into his flight bag. Air transportation is pretty democratic. Possibly too democratic; rare Japanese prisoners out-priority most passengers.

From time to time a red-headed first lieutenant came to the window of the D.A.T. office and announced over an asthmatic public address system: "All personnel for Horn Island (or Darwin or Moresby or Fall River or Archerfield)—when I call your name, answer and come up to the window and get your ticket and get in the truck next the taxiway. Hrrrmp. Captain Busyhead . . ." Four or

five names weren't answered to, in which cases the lieutenant repeated them in louder and angrier tones until some friend went off and dragged the offender away from his coffee and prunes in the A.R.C. canteen. In one case, where the recalcitrant customer, a staff sergeant named Foldfellow, Frederick L., was southbound, the lieutenant ad libbed, "Well, if you don't want your furlough, sergeant, I'll take it." This effort was rewarded with a barely perceptible ripple of laughter but probably wouldn't have been attempted had Foldfellow been a lieutenant colonel.

When the lieutenant called my name, we climbed aboard, sat or dozed for perhaps forty-five minutes until the pilot and crew showed up, took off without mishap and, following an uneventful flight over the Coral Sea, landed at Seven Mile. I was in New Guinea.

We unloaded. A thick, flat layer of heat settled over us. I wilted, visibly; so did a couple of other first arrivals. Somebody hailed a passing 2½ full of oxygen tanks that gave us a lift back to D.A.T. It was 1030 of a Tuesday. At 1045 of the same Tuesday I'd seen all

of New Guinea that I ever wanted to see and would willingly have boarded any southbound plane, debarked at Townsville and contented myself, for the rest of my life, with "Yeah, 1 just got down from Guinea," sidestepping any issues concerning how long I'd been there. I didn't like New Guinea. I don't like New Guinea. The romance is chiefly noticeable for perhaps ten minutes at dawn and again, for a similar period, when it isn't raining, at sunset. New Guinea dawns and sunsets, when half the sky is a screaming red pyre and even the dust over Jackson Strip takes on a pink glow, are probably among the world's more wondrous sights. But still far short of enticing any sane man to remain all night just to watch one.

As I closed, with half a dozen other soldiers, on a limp looking lister bag for a highly chlorinated drink of water that might remove

some of the gravel from my epiglotis, I was overcome with the kind of hopeless, sinking feeling that accompanies a flat tire and no spare on a deserted stretch of road, twenty-two miles from the nearest filling station. A badly rutted road ran parallel to the strip. Where the road wandered off into a welter of taxiways and revetments a dozen tents and three or four ambulances clustered around a large white sign: "First Air Evac." Upwards of two dozen battered, topless, mud splattered jeeps and 2½'s, one or two weapon-carriers and a lone command car were parked haphazardly along the road and between the road and the strip. Near the R.A.A.F. shack, more or less supported by a scarred, scrubby tree, was a ramshackle, Hooverville kind of establishment with a tin roof and canvas walls, that

101

sported a Red Shield (Salvation Army) banner. In it a thin Worker
was dispensing hot tea in used C-ration cans.

I availed myself of the Red Shield amenities and amused myself
with watching three Boongs (natives), the first I'd seen, who were
raking up the accumulated trash and debris that troops leave wherever they go. Two were dressed informally, in what looked like
dish towels; the third, whose hair was a startling shade of orange,
shuffled about on his flat black feet with a dirty pair of GI shorts
decorating his loins. "Here is the pristine savage in his native environment," I was telling myself when the character in the GIs dug

a crumpled pack of Luckies out of his waist band and—as blasé as a Harvard man with a briar—bummed a passing soldier for a light, lit, and inhaled deeply, with evident satisfaction.

The Moresby Road was a battered, pot-holed, half graveled, half surfaced track that curled along under a thick layer of dust and eighty odd kinds of Australian and American army vehicles, wound out of Moresby itself. The Moresby Road was the Main Stem; all life flowed along it. The dromes, in most cases, lay close on both sides of it, their taxiways crossed it, and thus, added to the hazards of dust, pot holes, galloping jeeps and Negro truck drivers (who have a propensity for swinging 2½'s full of high octane in and out and around traffic as they once swung their partners at the Savoy), were airplanes—24's, 17's, A-20's, 25's and '6's, 38's and 9's, 10's, 47's, transports. Coming suddenly, in a jeep, on a waddling B-24, with its four propellors whirling and a battery of .50-caliber machine guns protruding, leaves one with a decided feeling of inadequacy. In addition to the taxiways, which looked deceptively like roads except that they were generally better surfaced, numberless other tracks, trails and sideroads, few of which had a name, branched off the Moresby Road and wound up into the hills, crossing and re-crossing each other and the various strips until the maze would have

hopelessly stymied the most intelligent of lab-trained white mice. Over all this maze there was constant movement; ammunition convoys, gas and ration convoys, hitchhikers in profusion—Yank, Aussie, and Boong—a few battered staff cars sporting rear admiral's stars, Australian Bren Carriers, dusty jeeps full of dusty soldiers out to make Moresby in ten minutes flat (an impossible feat) and C-54's vied with each other for the right-of-way. From the air Port Moresby looked like a kind of huge, sprawling, mechanized ant hill, most of it "Made in the U.S.A." And it was almost inspiring, from the air.

From the ground it was *not* inspiring. Nor was I, as I trudged off and bummed my way to Advon Five in a jeep from the base chemical office, in the back of an Australian Malarial Control truck full of natives and fire extinguishers full of oil used in spraying

anopheles maternity wards, in a command car with an MP in a prime mover with a Negro and in another jeep. New Guinea, had there been any place to go, would have been a hitchhiker's paradise. I found my photographer friend, Richard, in the Advon public relations office, critically surveying a roll of negatives and cursing the

dampness that had ruined them. While I brought him up to date on the more hair-raising escapades the rest of our small staff had lately been embroiled in, he told me of the dull and miserable existence he'd been leading; then we carried my baggage down to the squadron EM area where Richard shared a tent with three other soldiers, including an ex Michigan state senator. I threw my barracks bag in a dirty wooden box that was to serve as a wardrobe, dressing table, hope chest and attic, and went off to see the squadron supply sergeant, who told me to come back after supper for a cot, mosquito bar and blankets. Then we went to supper.

The Advon messhall was a sprawling, clapboard and screen structure with a long line of soldiers hugging its scant shade like a living lei. Richard and I sweat the line for twenty-five minutes, eventually arriving, a foot at a time, at the entrance, a kind of airlock arrangement of screen doors that, it says here, kept the flies out. The lock cleared, a T/5 in kitchen-stained khaki pants and a greasy undershirt opened the outer door and ten or twelve of us crowded inside, where a sign stated: "No shorts in Messhall," and another, larger sign said, point blank: ATABRINZE. (I hadn't.) As the line inside the messhall dwindled away, the mess sergeant opened the inner door.

Supper that afternoon consisted of beefsteak, dehydrated potatoes, lima beans, bread, canned butter, GI coffee and a half-hearted kind of pudding made with butterscotch extract and varying amounts of water. This pudding, I was to learn, appeared on the menu regularly, usually twice a week, and varied in color, depending on the amount of water, from a pale lemon-yellow to near vermilion. The former tasted very, very faintly of butterscotch; the latter of more butterscotch than human beings are built to handle.

The menus that I speak of, incidentally, before anybody's ideas get out of hand, were not inserted smartly on individual tables between matched salt and pepper shakers, but were thumbtacked, one per day, on the bulletin board.

The most important part of our diet—the atabrine, vitamin and salt pills that graced a small shelf near the exit, with, now and then, a surly medic standing by to see that on that day at least the atabrine wasn't overlooked—didn't appear on the menu.

The quarters at Advon Five were drab, olive pyramidal tents, though most of them, in the course of time, had been improved by their occupants to an extent that would have made the F.H.A. turn green with envy. This technique of environment improvement, though not included or even mentioned in field manuals, is universally practiced and, at this late date, so highly developed an art that under-canvas comfort far exceeding the wildest dreams of the quartermaster corps is not uncommon. Practically all the tents at Advon were stretched over wooden frames, a trick that adds considerable head space. Most of them had floors, some of wood, some of crushed rock, some of steel strip-matting. The older inhabitants had elaborate slit trenches in their front yards. All had sundry racks, cupboards, tables and chairs made of salvaged metal, broken bucket seats, packing cases, tin, retired cots, scraps of lumber, and more strip-matting, which, with the 55-gallon gasoline drum, has pretty well replaced—in the Southwest Pacific at least—that great American fix-it—bailing wire. I doubt that there is a single Army kitchen in the theater, north of the 20th degree of latitude, that doesn't operate with the aid of a truckload of discarded 55-gallon drums and a quantity of matting.

The supply and first sergeants' tents, naturally, were on a par with most tourist cabins. Both had radios and electric lights and the supply sergeant's had an ice box. He lived with the mess sergeant and between them they formed an unbeatable combination. Other tents, wherein resided suburban types, were landscaped, surrounded by rows of little white rocks or struggling "Victory Gardens." The soil in the area was mostly clay, dust and gravel, a little inadequate for the more luxurious types of plant life; one tent, just behind ours, had nonetheless succeeded in enticing several stalks that looked like sunflowers to a height of about six feet. The shade these botanical question marks provided was of a more psychological than practical value. Our own tent, midst all this beauty, stuck out like a mangled

thumb, a glue factory in the middle of a zoning ordinance. The senator considered menial tasks beneath him, the other two occupants were sweating furloughs and beyond caring if the roof fell in, Richard and I were leaving shortly for the other side of The Hump and could see no point in instituting a lot of improvements that would chiefly benefit the senator. Consequently, our tent had no slit trench, sagged like a drunken sailor, wore sideburns of long wet grass that harbored several million mosquitoes, and was, inside, a clutter. The squadron CO occasionally drew this to our attention.

Our daily life in Moresby was fairly simple. After supper and a shower, if there was one, we sweat the "coke line"—a luxury of the highest order that had only just been instituted—for about 20 minutes or until we reached the PX. Where we handed our canteen cup to a soldier who splashed a shot of syrup in the bottom, then handed it to another soldier who filled it with carbonated water and handed it back to us. We stirred it with our mess spoon, tasted it, experimentally, to see whether we'd gotten too much syrup or too much carbonated water, then drank every drop, making it last as long as possible. Some soldiers could drag their coke binge out for nearly two hours, but it was debatable whether they gained more in pleasure than they lost through evaporation.

Following our pause that refreshed, four times a week, we went to the movies. Perhaps one in four of these would have gotten us out of the local pool room and into a theater in civilian life. From the remainder we would have stayed away in droves, and as far

away as possible. Why Hopalong Cassidy and Lupé Velez didn't win the Academy Award is beyond me. The shows were full of dialogue about as sparkling as Pidgin English, and conveyed in our general direction by characters formerly with the Walgreen circuit as bit players in a triple-decker-on-toast, but we could bet that by hook or by crook or the seat of their britches, they would somehow drag the War Effort, Remember Pearl Harbor and Old Glory into the finale. As Stateside audiences might leave on hearing there was a fire in the lobby, We the Audience left at this point and were generally well on our way home, mulling over in our minds, "WHAT is worth fighting for?" by the time the epic, with a final crescendo of sound and forty-eight chorines pealing "Oh Slap That

Jap!" fell flat on its face. "C'mon, less blow, they're goin' wave the flag," rippled through the audience as it became apparent that the leading man was about to step forward, leading with his chin, and against a background of crossed banners, the Capitol dome, Kate Smith's "God Bless America" and a massed chorus of belching war plant chimneys, tell us again what it was that WE were going to do to the Japs and the Axis. Certainly we went to these pictures; we walked miles and sat for hours, in rain or shine, to see them. We were essentially the same guys who laid 55 cents on the line at the box office in 1939; we wanted the same kind of 55 cent movies. Instead, seventy-five per cent of the time, we got tripe that should have been confined, and closely, to second-run penny arcades. The fact that these blunders opened with an announcement to the effect that the picture we were about to see had been prepared and released to the Armed Forces through the cooperation of the "The American Motion Picture Industry" added little to our love of the American Motion Picture Industry. It was like asking a man to appreciate the people who were going to hit him in the face with a dead herring.

Aside from the coke line and the breath of Hollywood, Moresby was a little bare of entertainment. When in Moresby proper we ate at the A.C.F. cafeteria, a barnlike structure that had somehow escaped damage during the Jap blitz. The cafeteria served regularly, neath palm fronds and crossed flags, canned tomato soup, roast beef or mutton, boiled (but real) potatoes, diced carrots and tea. This outlay was prepared by half a dozen stolid Boongs under the direction of an A.N.G.A.U. officer (Australian-New Guinea Administration Unit, responsible for native welfare in the Mandated Territory) and cost one-and-six or slightly less than two bits. The second cup of tea was free. When dining at the cafeteria it was necessary to bring your own knife and spoon. The cafeteria had only forks and at every meal either unaware of this fact or simply forgetful, a large proportion of the clientele could be seen drinking their soup, cutting their roast with two forks and considerable effort, and stirring their tea with a cookie.

Sunday afternoons we might visit a native village. Collecting our friend from the QM outfit, whose name was Schmaltz, we filled the rear of our jeep with battered canned goods unsuitable for U.S.

112

Army consumption, mostly salmon, and drove westward from Moresby for two hours, mostly in low gear, until an A.N.G.A.U. officer stopped us and told us the native villages were off limits. We knew this but hadn't known A.N.G.A.U. would be on the job, reminded him of the long drive we'd undergone to no avail, turned around and drove out of sight, then turned off across the fields and visited a native village anyway. Where we wound up stuck to the floorboards in a tidal flat. The village turned out en masse luckily, to push and pull and grunt and heave until we eventually got unstuck, then bargained with fish. Schmaltz, who had had experience in the line, handled our end of the business, called all the natives "chief," proffered each two cans of fish, and with his free arm backhanded the younger element who were trying to board us that they

might steal some fish. I made the mistake of lighting a cigarette in full view of the assembled populace and was lucky to get off with my life, let alone my cigarettes, the last of which a roly-poly little wench of perhaps three got off with. In the end we obtained three out-rigger canoe models that looked as if they should have been stamped "Made in Japan," at a cost of three cans of fish each. Schmaltz was a little chagrined at this price. "Some jerk," he said, "must have given them three cans for something. Everything will be three cans now. There's been a precedent set." Sociologically speaking, the natives may have been simple enough; economically they would have done well on Wall Street.

At 0600 next morning Richard and I, sated with the foibles and trappings of such civilization, went over The Hump with a load of cement, in a C-47 named "Old Kentuck." We landed at Dobodura. The original village, by the time Richard and I arrived, had been hopelessly and irretrievably lost to posterity, swallowed up by a bulldozer probably, and "Dobodura" applied to around a hundred and twenty square miles of New Guinea, splotched with jungle and Kunai flats and literally crawling with roads, airstrips, taxiways, revetments and the United States Army. Dobo's growth, when we arrived, had gotten to the stage where unit commanders were posting guards, lest some overzealous engineers one bright day drive a road through the officer's latrine, and truck drivers dared not close their eyes against the thick suffocating smother of clogging white dust that blanketed all of Dobodura lest, opening them, they found themselves and their truck in the middle of a brand new airstrip, flying formation with two big Libs.

After supper we went to the movie. The theater was in the middle of a large Kunai flat not far from a string of revetments that were huddled at one end of a fighter strip, had a roof and that was about all. The sides and ends were naught but poles, but the roof (of canvas) served to cover the screen, a projection booth built of scrap lumber and perhaps a sixth of the soldiers who attended early, provided they came early enough. The remaining five-sixths sat outside on the hoods and fenders and cabs of their vehicles. Everybody brought their own seats. The plot unwound smoothly enough until midway of the second reel, when it stopped, abruptly. Above the groans of the audience a voice from the projection booth said: "Yellow Alert!" Richard and I clutched the boxes we were sitting on convulsively. Nobody else moved; the rest of the audience only muttered. The soldier next to me mouthed obscene words that informed us that the bastards had interrupted the movie the night before with six of their alerts. The voice from the booth went on: "All ack-ack crews report to your guns. No smoking and keep them car lights off. We'll run the movie unless it's a Red Alert." The audience muttered their approval and "Murder" took up, jerkily. Perhaps five minutes went by. Richard and I had gradually relaxed and eased our bottoms back on our boxes when, suddenly, a 20-mm gun barked three times. The screen went dark. The voice said: "Red Alert! Scatter out, away from the theater area! We'll start the show again when it's over." The muttering, this time, was louder and more profane. The audience arose and taking their boxes with them, filtered into the Kunai. Nobody appeared to be in any great hurry except Richard and me, who left the area quite rapidly indeed and kept going until we came across a drainage ditch partially full of water. Half a dozen other soldiers presently joined us, and sat or lay beside the ditch. Overhead a great, round moon beamed down. I'm not sure about Richard, but I was scared, and I felt exceptionally conspicuous. And I thought some, fleetingly, of home; and thought, too, that in relation to the size of all Dobodura my own thin frame offered a rather poor target and probably stood small mathematical chance of sustaining a direct hit. This, however, wasn't too reassuring. Thus we sat for perhaps ten minutes, when WHAM! A 20-mm barked!

A lanky soldier who had been sitting beside me, surreptitiously sucking on a cigarette, helped me out of the drainage ditch and informed me that one shot meant "All Clear." We went back to the theater, found the inside full and the heroine's song completed (it's an ill wind . . .) and settled for a seat on the hood of a GI truck that offered a relatively unobstructed view of slightly less than three-quarters of the screen. "Murder" wound along for another reel and a half, until a second Red Alert stopped the hero dead, on the verge of his greatest triumph. We repeated the ditch routine just as heartily as the first time, which was more than most of the audience did, and returning after the all clear, got seats in deep left field. The

116

third Red Alert brought with it a realization that, at long last, *I* knew what I was fighting for: I had learned to hate the Japanese.

Next morning we rode to Oro Bay in a jeep named "Mud, Sweat and Gears." From five miles at sea Oro Bay had all the romantic requisites of a South Sea Island postcard—a dazzling sweep of white beach backed by slim graceful palm trees and fronted by a foaming line of surf. Closer inspection revealed that the American Army had pretty effectively shattered the postcard possibilities by building latrines at frequent intervals along the beach. These were simply ten-foot-square platforms perched high upon stakes driven into the sea bottom and mounting boxlike arrangements whose plumbing consisted of six or eight holes. A narrow wooden walk, much like a lake resort jetty, connected each with the beach. Occupants were, of course, awfully exposed to all who passed through Oro Bay or crossed the Pacific. They were very drafty.

Our arrival at the Bay was somewhat overshadowed by the arrival, a couple of hours later, of the first contingent of nurses ever to grace Oro. Their presence created an understandable stir and led to a noticeable increase in shoe polish sales at the officer's PX, and a great scurry on the part of various unit commanders that resulted in the hasty addition of burlap screening to the aforesaid latrines. Thanks to the Army Nurse Corps, Richard and I remained at Oro Bay four days, more or less unnoticed.

On the third night we saw Judy Garland in "Me and My Gal," for the third time. Two Red Alerts replaced the short features. It was during one of them, while sharing the edge of a hole with another soldier, that I attained a new stature. Both of us, during the first few minutes of the alert, had devoted ourselves, alternately, to saying some prayers and cursing the moon, but no Bettys (Japanese medium bombers) appearing, we knocked that off and struck up a conversation. It developed that my companion had been in Oro Bay but two days. He intimated that that was plenty.

"Yeah?" I said, "You shoulda been here when it was *really* tough. Before . . . before there were any nurses."

I had come "over The Hump"—physically, mentally, and spiritually.

When Richard and I presented ourselves at the Water Transport Office the forenoon of our fourth day in Oro, a sergeant told us, "I think I can get you on a small ship to Morobe this afternoon. Be down here at 12:30, ready to go." Richard and I knew only that Morobe was a place fairly well up the northeast New Guinea coast in the general direction of Salamaua. By the time we had boarded our small ship we'd learned from a soldier that it was "a hot spot," a scheduled stop for the Japanese Air Force and the recent recipient of nine Jap raids in eight days.

Our small ship was a coastal vessel of the type that Zeros sink in passing, much as small boys squash caterpillars. In its vitals it had some kind of an engine and a crew of five. However, the engineer alone weighed "seventeen bloody stone," a good part of it tattooed and most of it in view, since he wore only a grease-stained pair of GI shorts and a battered pair of black oxfords without laces. Scarcely had we clambered over the side when the master shouted down the companionway to Sam, the A.N.G.A.U. boy, to brew up another billy of tea for the Yanks.

That night I slept reasonably well on the hatch cover, wrapped in a poncho, and next morning woke to learn that the handful of lumpy little islands dead ahead marked the entrance to Morobe harbor.

Morobe was essentially an Australian base, but sitting behind a packing case in the Movement Control Office were two Yanks, who obligingly disclosed the infrequency of departures from the port.

They were right, for not so much as an outrigger canoe left all day. At intervals two L.C.V.P.s backed resolutely off the beach, their motors roaring. At intervals we leaped hopefully to our feet, like so many applicants in a mid-depression employment agency. As the Vs throttled down and returned to the beach, we throttled down and sank back on our mail sacks.

We watched, too, for the Jap planes, until a KP explained that you didn't watch the sky, you watched the A.N.G.A.U. boys rolling gas drums aboard an L.C.T. Like canary birds in a coal mine they had a sixth sense that warned of the approach of danger long before the system's yellow alert. The Boongs would look apprehensively skyward, roll their eyes a couple of times, drop their gas drums like hot rocks and depart for the ridge.

As we finished eating dinner, our errant KP reappeared and asked us over to his tent. There we were introduced to a half a dozen soldiers lying on cots mid a welter of scattered clothing and equipment. We learned that they were from the tank-destroyer battalion of a U.S. infantry division, which was then fighting south of Salamaua. Dropped in Morobe for the purpose of trans-shipping supplies, they had, they were positive, been forgotten. Their mail wandered in aimlessly, weeks older than usual; so did rumors of the rest of the battalion's return to Australia. They had been bombed repeatedly, but worse than that, they had had to subsist on Australian field rations, as the American-made supplies they'd handled had consisted mostly of blood plasma and ammunition. The nifty little tinned dainty of the Australian Army is dehydrated mutton—excellent for keeping a barracks bag off the wet ground, but hardly for internal use.

Yet there was one star gleaming bright in their murky sky. It seems that a month or so ago a 55-gallon drum had arrived in the middle of a shipment of 105-mm. howitzer shells and barbed wire. Unmarked it was and unnamed, apparently unwanted, and after three days unclaimed. Its contents? Medical alcohol. They welcomed it warmly and took it in. Now there was a little less than two gallons left, and several of the boys had taken on a somewhat bluish tinge.

We sat down and exchanged the customary "whereyafrominthestates?" and "whatwereyadoinforethewar?" Two of them, it soon developed, were in the same fraternity as I. Naturally this got the afternoon off to a flying start. As I watched one of my Brothers measure a pinch of J-ration lemon powder and two fingers of 190-proof medical alcohol into a canteen cup half full of chlorinated water, I could but admire the international scope of our organization.

We toasted each other. It started raining, softly, monotonously. Now there is something about the combination of a gray day, persistent rain and medical alcohol that induces philosophical discussions of the world's problems, be the philosophers in Morobe or North Red Wing, Minnesota. Our philosophy seemed, like our po-

tion, 190 proof. Having pretty well covered the uglier facets of our
friends' later lives we went on—to the home front labor situation, as
so frequently is the case. To be sure most of our information was
culled from Australian newspapers of the month before, but what
we had heard didn't make sense. Our own lives, from a coldly
monetary point of view, we agreed, were worth an average of about
$75 a month; that 2½¢ an hour one way or the other could make
much difference to anybody was beyond us. That *any* strike might
conceivably be justified was likewise beyond us. Their merits be
damned, wartime strikes, we decided, were like arguing about a
leaky stateroom faucet during a shipwreck: In normal times a leaky
faucet might rate a certain priority—not now. Strikes, in our opinion, were simply making of the whole business of World War II a
three-way tug-of-war, with us, somehow, on the short end of the
rope. In this respect we perhaps had the advantage of Stateside folk
in that we were on the ground where we could see, all too plainly,

just how short our rope was. That 7700 field ranges were needed by the armed forces was perhaps slightly more than astounding to our Stateside friends. And to our Stateside friends the news that a minor walkout in one of the plants manufacturing those 7700 ranges would, it was hoped, be ironed out during a conference on the following Monday and had, at any rate, so a plant official stated, decreased production by only one half of one per cent, might almost be construed as encouraging. To us that one half of one per cent was the field range we didn't have. Our lack of field ranges we blamed, of course, almost entirely on John L. Lewis. Were Mr. Lewis of a somewhat less purposeful nature and in a position to sit in on one such discussion as ours, I sometimes think—or at least I like to think—that following same he might drop quietly down a deep hard shaft, without benefit of portal-to-portal pay.

In all probability, of course, about the time our muster-out payments cease and most of us are again in the enviable position of considering a $2\frac{1}{2}$ ¢ per hour wage cut as a more frightening possibility than the loss of any of our lives or limbs, we'll back labor heart and soul; but after three or four or five years service many of us, in spite of our claiming throughout those three or four or five years that we are simply "civilians in uniform," may well be something akin to professional soldiers.

In our discussion of the production problem, we did not, as in most such forums, begin with a statement to the effect that American labor has done, on the whole, a magnificent job. That we expected, as a Big 10 coach expects blocking and, like Big 10 coaches, we only bawled the holy, living hell out of those who, in our opinion, weren't blocking.

As it grew dark we lit candles and finished the lemon powder while listening to a battered phonograph, covered with green mold, playing over and over half a dozen warped records.

Richard and I spent the night with our friends and left Morobe at 0930 next morning, somewhat the worse for too much lemon powder, in an L.C.V.P., Amphibian Engineer manned, bound for Nassau Bay with a load of 105-mm. pack-howitzer parts. Thus began, for us, two weeks of practical beachcombing. We beat our way up the coast via L.C.V.P., L.C.M., L.C.T., small ship, shanks

mare, and—once in a while—wheeled transportation. From beach to bay to inlet to cove to beach again until we'd reach a point twelve miles east of Lae. Then back to Buna.

Nassau Bay, Tambu Bay, Roosevelt Ridge, Dot Inlet, Salamaua, Monoghan's Beach, Lae Jetty, Red Beach, Yellow Beach, Yellow Beach Two, the Boxoo, the Booso, Malahang Plantation. Sounds like the mutterings of a tired geodetic surveyor.

127

We slept here and there and anywhere, and almost always in our clothes. Sometimes we just crouched in holes while the Japanese aircraft droned overhead—more nuisance than menace.

Once we'd just strung our hammocks from the remnants of a Jap barbed-wire entanglement. I'd best explain that our hammocks were of the jungle type, GI issue, made of about equal parts of rubberized canvas, mosquito netting and rope. Erected as shown in field manuals they would have been fine, I'm sure. We soon found, however, that the trees and shrubs around Huon Gulf had somehow received very little training in where and how far apart to grow to be of the slightest use in erecting a jungle hammock in accordance with field manual standards. It was easier if we just lay our hammocks flat on the ground like sleeping bags. It would have been easier still if each had been accompanied by the issue of one small boy to carry it. But the easiest thing of all was to throw our hammocks away and sleep in our ponchos. Which eventually we did.

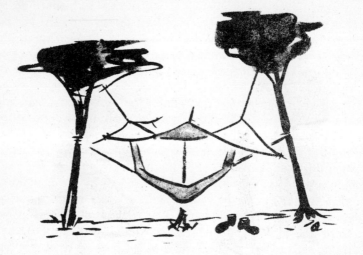

We still had our hammocks, however, that night at Salamaua and had erected them and crawled inside and were sleeping pretty decently—until the rain came. Lightly at first, leading a slight breeze that only sifted a certain wetness through my mosquito netting, it presently came harder and faster and harder and faster, and I realized

that I had pitched my hammock in a slight depression. For about twenty minutes I fought a losing battle, of the kind that brought fame to a small Dutch customer, but confronted with more leaky dykes than fingers, wound up lying in four inches of cold, rapidly rising water, suspecting the tide had come in. I gave up then, unzipped my hammock—at about the same time somebody unzipped a similiar contraption in the sky above, releasing great bucketfuls of rain.

So far as I knew there were no buildings with roofs left standing in Salamaua, and what I expected to gain by splashing around in the rain and the blackness I don't know, but I knew I could get no wetter unless I walked off a pier. I walked or waded for perhaps a mile, when during a blue flash of lightning I saw, just off the road, the gaping remains of a building and hanging on it a wet, muddy, bedraggled "American Red Cross" banner. I was in no mood to consider what my contributions to past community chest drives might merit in return; I splashed over to the building and felt for a door. Inside a flashlight blinked and a sleepy voice yelled, "Who's there?"

"St. George," I yelled back, which probably enlightened them not at all, "Can I sleep here?"

The voice muttered and there were sounds of somebody untangling blankets. The voice said, "Here's a blanket," then swore again as the flashlight fell on the floor and went out. I clutched the

blanket; the voice said, "Come over here, where you are there isn't
any roof." I lurched through the blackness, mumbled something
about I certainly appreciated the hospitality. Then the voice said,
"Not near the wall. Over here. Where you are there isn't any
floor." I rolled my blanket about me and went to sleep.

We ate what we could, when we could—usually out of cans or
boxes and occasionally out of messkits. Let me tell you right here
that without the ungrudging generosity of the Diggers—the overwhelming generosity of all the A.I.F.—Richard and I would have
led considerably less comfortable lives than we did.

I remember a certain meal that came on top of eighty-four hours
without anything more in the way of food than the gutted remains
of some J-rations. We'd been riding since early morning on a ¾-ton
weapons carrier whose driver was looking for a lost bulldozer, and
still is for all I know. We had done seventeen miles over a new
corduroy road that wound through the back country toward Mala-

hang Plantation. We'd given a lift to a P.I.B. boy and he stayed with us until we bogged down to the hubs the third time. Then he started hiking and when we caught up with him declined our renewed offer by saying "Me walk," and nothing more. The road angled seaward and petered out; so the driver decided to turn back. By that time our empty stomachs were draped over our pelvi.

Casting about we found two broken cases of bully beef. We fell on these, scavenged a can each and asked of a passing Digger, a lance-jack lugging a canvas bucket full of water, did he have anything to open them with? The soul of friendliness and generosity, as were all the Diggers we met along those beaches, he said, "Yer roight, Yank, follow me." We followed him back into the jungle bordering the beach, where the rest of his gun crew—they had a Bofors 20 in position near the water's edge—were stashing some rations they had scrounged. One of them opened our bully with a jack knife. In return we offered cigarettes. "Yer got plenty?" they asked, hesitating to our amazement. We assured them we had and they accepted. "First bloody smoke I've 'ad in a week," one of them said. Hearing that, we offered the remainder of the pack, and the Diggers, not to be outdone, pressed on us a can of black currant jam and a box of biscuits and told us: "Yer go back up ther bloody track, Yank, there's a Salvation bloke wot'll give yer some tea." We went off with our bully and biscuits and tea and found the Salvation bloke, who filled our canteen cups with tea and let us heat our bully

in his coals. When the little white lumps of fat that are a feature of bully beef were oozing, we raked the cans out of the fire, opened our jam with a bayonet, spread thick gobs of bully beef and black currant jam on our biscuits and ate ravenously, washing the whole mess down with great swallows of hot, unsweetened tea. We burnt our fingers on the bully cans and wound up greasy, sticky with jam to our elbows, and covered with ashes and blisters. It was as fine a meal as I ever hope to eat.

As for the Salvation Army, Richard and I have come to the conclusion that that organization's workers, attached to the A.I.F., land with the leading elements of the first assault wave, complete with billy, tea, biscuits and banner and prepared to go into business at the drop of a bomb that will clear them a crater. They were always there. Later, as we were wondering audibly as to where and in what we would sleep that night, an Australian lance-jack came crawling through the undergrowth, hissing, "Simon, Billy, Jocko . . . ?" One of the Diggers said, " 'Ell, Yank, yer can sleep in our beds, we're unloadin' the bloody barges all night." We accepted that offer, too.

Once we met a character, for instance, near Lae, whose worldly possessions consisted of: a Jap loin cloth, a wet handkerchief tied around his head, his Enfield and a bandolier of ammunition, and a cup. He seemed perfectly happy. The sun was warm, he could defend himself or kill, his cup assured him of food, and he could, he seemed satisfied, scrounge some clothes, possibly some shoes, even a poncho before the day was over ... "So wot the bloody 'ell?" And we met another Digger, in the flattened remains of Lae proper. He was sitting in the shade of a piece of corrugated tin he'd propped up, watching a billy of tea brewing over a small fire with one eye, and, with the other, so help me, reading a copy of *Gone With The Wind* that he'd found among the wreckage. Beside our Digger, neatly wrapped and sewed in some dead Jap's belly band, were two small boxes addressed to a Mrs. Henry Something, Bondi, Sydney, N.S.W., that contained a complete silver tea set, in "bloody good repair" and embossed with the anchors of the Imperial Japanese Navy. This set he had also found in the wreckage and carefully packaged for "his missus" before turning to "GWTW," unmindful of the occasional rattle of Bren guns on the far side of the town, where a handful of glory-bound Japs were holding out behind bunkers of 55-gallon drums filled with dirt.

Such *sang froid* can only be acquired, not taught.

And wherever we went we heard, over and over, endlessly, day in and day out, on beaches and on barges, the perennial bitches of the U.S. Army abroad—"Been nine goddam months in Guinea . . . lousy chow . . . goddam officers . . . when are we going home . . ." and so on, ad infinitum. The A.I.F. we met, after three years of Greece, Crete, Tobruk and El Alemein, had seen so much and survived so much and had so many close calls that another close call more or less was simply a part of the day's work of killing. They were very tough cookies; but said little or nothing about it. Our own troops must have bored the A.I.F. immensely. And the A.I.F. had learned—or at least become resigned—to getting along without. They complained, of course, but on the whole they were inclined to make the best of things. They knew better than to expect anything more. Not so we Yanks, who were apparently unable to forget, for even a minute, that someplace in the world there were people sleeping warmer and dryer than we were.

We are still bitching our heads off, though, and I've come to the conclusion that Americans, simply, are not—and will never be—satisfied. Probably it is what makes us the country we are. What other nation sends crushed pineapple into a beachhead on D-plus-2?

THEN I RETURNED to the mainland and "the best damn city" to have my malaria.

"The fever" used to be the occupational disease of the Southwest Pacific. Some old timers can bend elbows and tell you about twenty-four recurrent attacks. What with the Japanese corner on the world's quinine, it would be still except for atabrine. Atabrine's virtues are extolled by the sub-equatorial roadside much as Burma Shave used to be in the States' automobile days, and in much the same phraseology.

In the more northerly parts, where malaria is endemic, control officers spend eight hours daily reminding the balance of the forces of that fact, and in some bases the absence of a shirt is a court martial offense. What with the anopheles billed as Public Enemy No. 1, prevention requires no individual effort. But back on the central Mainland getting atabrine entailed a walk of two blocks, and I had to remember by myself about swallowing one each day. So it got me.

For about a week I spent a fair share of each day hooped over a knee-high electric heater, singeing my forelock while a raft of per-

SCARCELY A MAN –

IS NOW ALIVE –

YOU SEE...

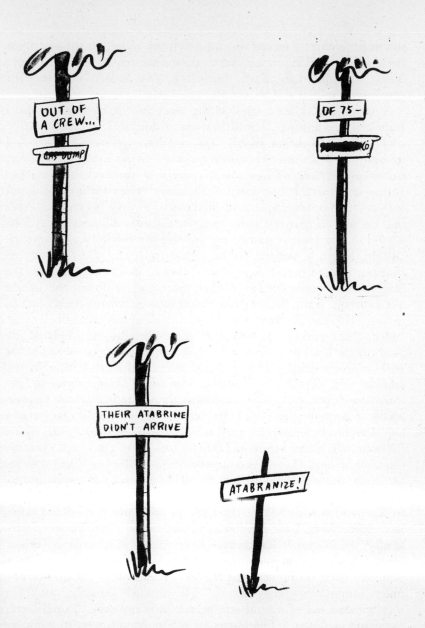

sistent little chills shivered up and down my spine. In the end I got tired of my striking resemblance to a discouraged zombie I once knew, and turned in at the dispensary. My malaria was now the responsibility of the U.S. Army.

A rather pretty little trick at the reception desk asked me did I want to see someone? I told her yes, a doctor, I thought I had a touch of malaria. She asked, "Do you have a Form 52 here?" I thought not but wasn't very sure about it—Army records sometimes follow soldiers around like a bad reputation—until she asked me had I been in before. I told her no. She said, "Then I'll make one out for you," and producing a three-inch pad of Form 52's extracted from me, bit by bit, that my name was St. George, Thomas R., A.S.N. 37097130, my rank corporal, my age 24, my birthplace Minnesota, and my length of service, to the closest full year, two. These vital statistics pleased her. She put my Form 52 in a small box near the surgery door and told me go over there and sit down, the doctor will call you. I sat. Perhaps ten minutes passed, then a hand reached through the door, extracted my Form 52, disappeared again; a voice called, "St. George?" I answered "Here" briefly and followed my 52 through the door, where a Captain, Medical Corps, looked at me with a professionally fishy eye and asked me what I thought my trouble was. I told him malaria. He said, "Mmmmmmmm," returned my card, and said I should go across the hall where Captain Miles or Biles or Files (I didn't catch the name) would take care of me. I went obediently across the hall, explained who I was, where I'd been, who'd sent me on and what it was I thought I had. Another Captain, Medical Corps (presumably Miles or Biles or Files) told me sit down, and a nurse who was puttering around with some instruments paused in passing and plugged a thermometer into my face. In accordance with S.O.P., the Captain promptly turned and asked me: "Little fever, huh? Mmmmmm. Had chills? Feel rundown generally? Head ache? Backache? Eyes tired? Had malaria before? How long have you been down here? When did you leave New Guinea? Been taking atabrine lately?" I told him, "Glugh—uckle—mlerf—nerg—dlut—glerg—blereh." He nodded absently, took the thermometer out of my mouth, peered at it and said, "You'd better go in and lie down." The nurse left off stacking towels to point me through a door and into a small, darkened room full of hospital beds. I crawled onto one and pulled off my tie.

About 7:15 a T-5 came in and asked, "You going to the hospital?" I said I guessed so. He said, "Okay, they's a car here." Three of us left the dispensary, climbed into a staff car and were whisked through the early evening to the 118th General.

The OD there said, "Mmmmmmm. Now, do you want to check your valuables?" I gathered that it was the custom, so left with him the bulk of my ready cash, a check for $10 and a postal money order for $25. It seemed a shame, somehow, that I couldn't produce in the way of valuables some kind of heavy jade ring, but the OD overcame any disappointment he may have felt and listed cheerfully enough, on MD Form 25-dash-something, my rather prosaic possessions.

I went to bed then and dozed until a tall, red-headed ward boy showed up and though I was but half awake, took out of my left forearm 10 cc of blood that I could ill afford to spare. "For your smear," he said.

In all I spent seven days in Ward 15, most of them extremely restful and even pleasant. At 10:30 the morning after my admittance I was examined by the ward doctor. He gave me the usual treatment—prodding me fore and aft and listening to my interior thumpings, I breathed deeply, said "Ahhhh," inhaled, exhaled and repeated my symptoms. My examination completed, the captain prescribed "the

treatment" and I went back to bed. Herman blew in about noon (he was still in town and I had phoned him) with my razor and toothpaste, a dribble of mail and some snide remarks about goldbricking.

The particular treatment that I was undergoing seldom interfered with my pleasure since it consisted simply of swallowing atabrine tablets on schedule. During the first seventy-two hours of the treatment, of course, some of the atabrine swallowing occurred in the dead of night. On these occasions the night nurse came around, at 0200 and again at 0600 on the first night, asked me if I was St. George—all we snoring bundles no doubt looked pretty much alike —and satisfied that I was, pressed two atabrine tablets into my one hand, a paper cup full of water into my other, and shined her flashlight in my face. I was never more than a fifth awake at the time, but would somehow contrive to get one tablet into my mouth and one down my pajama front, spill most of the water over my chin, and still muttering, go back to sleep.

In addition to the atabrine, at odd moments during the day (about every 15 minutes or so, it seemed) a nurse turned up, caught us unawares and popped a thermometer into our mouths. If questioned directly ("Am I normal?") and pressed she would sometimes admit that yes, we were "normal," but she preferred to keep this information locked deep in her own starched bosom. Some of the older patients could with commendable ease talk around their thermometers and thus passed each day a few pleasant moments, bandying rep artees with Lt. Peters, but I never mastered this feat nor even attempted it, lest I wind up swallowing several cc of mercury and some powdered glass. I did learn, though, that a glass of water just previous to having my temperature taken would sometimes lower the results by as much as a .5 of a degree. Lt. Peters knew this too, however, and I doubt that my chart was ever much affected.

Pleasant as it was, my hospitalization, after the first few days, began to wear thin. My fever subsided, I felt practically virile, and after writing all the people I owed letters and reading the limited supply of available literature, except a number of comic books, I was ready to leave. Say on about the third day. This, of course, was unthinkable; I was "for" the treatment and the treatment I would get, come hell or high water. Get it I did, though each morning, from the third day on, I told the Captain on his morning rounds that I was "Fine!" with increasing enthusiasm and even suggested that I might turn handsprings in the aisle to prove it. The Captain only smiled and nodded and passed on. My enforced rest grew increasingly tiresome. Some of the soldiers in Ward 15 had apparently become resigned to spending the rest of their natural lives there and appeared content enough; others steamed and stewed as I did. In either case, as is the custom with Army hospitals, on attaining a state of health that left us incapable of bashing our spines for more than ten hours at a stretch, we were put to light work. On one occasion I aided in washing the dinner dishes, on Saturday afternoon four of us cleaned the windows, again I was detailed to the patients' mess for a half day to cut up beans. None of these tasks was in itself very arduous, but they seemed to add weight to the belief, widely held by soldiers, that no one is ever discharged from an Army hospital until the authorities therein are thoroughly satisfied that he has paid for his bed, board and treatment in kind. This is probably not altogether true. If it is, the authorities, in my case, were badly short changed. My labors, at 40 cents an hour, would scarcely have paid for the thermometers I swallowed. Possibly the authorities realized that I was a losing proposition. At any rate, on the seventh day I was discharged, feeling far healthier than I had for eight months before or have since, and in time to meet the first WACs to grace our theater.

SOME SERIOUS CONSIDERATION OF THE WACS *

Now THE RUMOR that "300 (or 500 or 700 or 900) WACs are gonna' land next week" was one of the best rumors the Southwest Pacific ever had. First heard in the early Stateside summer of 1943— some months after WACs *had* landed in North Africa—it persisted, like recurrent malaria, for nearly a year, until May 1944, when roughly 500 WACs did land. Five WAC officers had landed earlier, in March, but we took little notice of them except as an omen. They were, after all, still "officer's stuff." We were waiting for the EWs (Enlisted Women). We had never seen a WAC, and our imaginations were incapable of coping with the picture of American girls—gay, irresponsible, irrepressible, irresistible creatures that we remembered them—as GI, in uniforms, abiding by the A.R.s and A.W.s and *all wearing the same clothes*.

So it was that a photographer named Marvin and I, armed with press cards, a special dock pass, cameras and relatively open minds, showed up at pier 7, Woolloomooloo, at 12:30 of a May afternoon, the second anniversary of our own arrival, prepared to meet the WACs. Or rather, unprepared. On hand for the event, in addi-

* The serious implications of this chapter become apparent from one of Ozzie's letters: "However, I'm engaged (to be married!) to a dark-eyed, saucy little girl from Philadelphia, presently a S/Sgt. in the WACs—it's serious."

tion, were a Navy shore party of perhaps two hundred sailors, an A.M.F. dock detail numbering another hundred, approximately a battalion of MPs turned out in their finest, the Base Seven military band, the Base CO (a BG) and his staff, several Australian brigadiers, an odd dozen rather horsefaced women representing the WAAAFs, WRANs, AWAMS and so on, a few longshoremen, and the rest of the assembled press, both Australian and American, including, naturally, a number of newsreel men who had deserted the fighting fronts to cover the WACs.

The ship on which several hundred WACs were alleged cargo hove in sight in the outer reaches of the bay about one o'clock. Some thirty minutes later, when a farsighted eye might with luck have distinguished a ventilator from a 5-inch gun, somebody yelled, "There's one!" A murmur of anticipation rippled through the crowd. As the shout, "There's one!" was heard at pretty regular intervals during the ensuing hour and a half that it took the ship to near the dock, this murmur was repeated. Eventually three honest-to-goodness WACs were seen, in all their glory, on an upper deck. Everybody joined in a ragged, spontaneous cheer. It might have been a milestone in our war, but by the white painted bars on their helmets we knew these WACs as officers, and a thin sailor voiced the general sentiment when he bellowed, *"Where are the privates?"* Then somebody saw two heads—female heads—jammed in a porthole amidships. By their position (amidships, low down) we knew them for EWs. There was another spontaneous cheer. Behind us an MP, in the voice of one making a great discovery, gurgled, "That's a WAC! Hear her *laugh!"* Other heads, WAC heads ("Sure it's a WAC, you can tell by her hair!") appeared in other amidships portholes. One's hair was red. "Ooooooh RED!" screamed not more than 300 of the assembled gobs and GIs. Somebody yelled, "Anybody there from Ohio?" The ship bumped against the pier, a lieutenant (jg) ordered, "Shore party aft!" The band struck up "The Star Spangled Banner." The United States of America have seldom seemed closer than at that moment.

A gangplank was presently rigged, the BG and his staff and certain other dignitaries went aboard. They returned to the dock, somebody hauled up with a wreath, slightly smaller than those awarded Kentucky Derby winners, and a sign: "Welcome WACs."

The stage was set. Two WACs, a captain and a Pfc., appeared at the top of the gangplank. The band struck up something, a volley of flashbulbs popped—a little prematurely, it turned out. The captain and the Pfc. were Signal Corps WACs and were coming ashore first that they might shoot pictures of the other WACs debarking. The press, however, closed on them regardless, as they reached the foot of the gangplank, and bore them away, each the center of a small eddy of the Fourth Estate asking, "What's your name? Where are you from in America? What did you do before you joined?" The Pfc., who was an Englishwoman and thirty-eightish and had joined to settle a Blitz score, had her glasses knocked slightly askew, got separated from her captain, and was in all, I think, a little confused by the demonstration. Until the troop commander aboard ship, a Major (WAC) appeared at the top of the gangplank, the BG cleared his throat, the band struck up again, and the press surged back as near the gangplank as a cordon of MPs would let them. The captain and the Pfc. straightened their helmets, tugged at their trenchcoats, and turning toward the gangplank, started popping flashbulbs as industriously as anybody. An indication, that.

145

The troop commander aboard ship ventured down the gangplank and was engulfed by the welcoming committee. She came up with the wreath in one hand, shaking hands all around with the other. A few salutes were tossed. The BG made a short speech, officially welcoming her and the WACs to the Southwest Pacific, and possibly —the general was known as "Not a bad old guy" around the Base Seven N.C.O. club—offering a few words of encouragement. Which, I suspect, the Major may have appreciated. The Major was followed ashore by the remaining WACs, officers first—there were perhaps a hundred, mostly captains and lieutenants—and then, at long last, GI WACs.

Our WACs, in helmets, raincoats, and the WAC version of a full field pack, looked short, dumpy, healthy and surprisingly efficient, remarkably like so many well-fed, reliable White Leghorns.

A captain standing next me expressed our surprised sentiments when he exclaimed, "My God! GI shoes!"

146

DURING MY MONTHS as a Mainland Fat Cat our theater had increased in length by about two thousand miles. The American Red Cross being pretty well established along a fair share of that distance I sallied forth myself, headed north—and remained relatively speechless for a period of thirty days. The changes left me that way. Our shoestring war was over.

There were more planes and consequently more priorities, and two of us, picking up our travel orders at the AG's office left via air the following morning. Reaching Brisbane we found a covey of staff cars waiting at the airport. One of them carried us—just the two of us and not a commission between us—downtown. By noon we'd made the rounds of the offices. They said, "We'll fix you up," and phoned back in mid-afternoon to say we were leaving on ATC at 0900 next morning. A year previously Richard and I had cooled our heels in Brisbane for a matter of ten days more or less, and a couple of weeks later been reduced to riding a glider.

We were further impressed with the improvement at Townsville where we RON'd (Remained Overnight) because of weather. (The weather was still reliably unreliable.) A truck met our plane at Tville as it taxied to a halt. Shades of Pan American. Transportation for less than a full colonel! No longer had we transients to rely on our thumbs and the good graces of truck drivers.

Townsville itself, and it struck me as might the loss of an old friend, was practically deserted. The bitter, sweating hordes of Yanks who had once clogged its blistering streets had migrated northward in the space of about three months. To such an extent that girls, in twos and threes, walked the streets, *alone.*

Port Moresby, where we lay over about an hour sweating some weather on The Hump, was a veritable ghost town. Its brown hills were bare. The only traces of the forgotten GI civilization that had once churned those hills to dust were the deserted, rubble-strewn campsites they'd left behind them, stripped clean as if by locusts by the scrounge-minded Boongs. As we circled for a landing the flat, naked slabs of cement that had once floored mess halls, offices, Ops shacks, EM clubs, O's clubs, all crawling with Yanks, stared up at us like blank faces. Nothing is as desolate as a deserted base, left behind in the march of war.

On Moresby's lone operational strip an American Red Cross canteen, at long last, served, lo and behold! bread and butter *and* jam, to anybody, no matter which way they were going.

Over Dobodura, where once, short months before, planes had hovered over fifteen odd operational strips like moths around a street light, a scant half dozen ships wheeled forlornly in a deserted sky.

In Nadzab a couple of the signs of our times on two latrines opened wide with amazement my innocent blue eyes. On one the sign read: "MEN Officers Enlisted Men." On the other "WOMEN Officers Enlisted Personnel." My aching back! A milestone, the death knell of that time-worn New Guinea lament, "Ain't seen a white women in thirteen months."

And there were other signs. In Nadzab the air strips were no longer ringed with revetments like great, gray dirty jello molds. We, now, held air superiority, and our planes were parked, nonchalantly, wing tip to wing tip, in plain sight on hardstands. A small point perhaps, but it cheered me.

Nadzab, where we remained a few days, was itself in the process of folding, fast folding, as had Moresby and Dobodura before it, and almost perceptibly, each day, the population decreased before our very eyes. Visiting an NCO club of an evening we might hear from various members, "Yeah, we're moving out pretty soon. Biak I guess." Revisiting the club a week later, we might well find nothing, not so much as a bottle cap. Our friends in the interim had moved out, torn down their club, struck their tents, rolled up the burlap and screening and tarpaulins, struck sometimes the very frameworks of their messhall and offices, packed up their signs and gas drums and showers and latrines and volley ball nets and gone. Where? The grapevine would tell us exactly where soon enough.

The mess, in a year's time, had so improved that I felt much as might a man who had died during the heydey of broiled venison and hominy grits and returned to this earth for a quick snack at the automat. At four meals a week, sometimes, there was fresh butter!

It was, I guess, the passable edibility and wider variety of foods prepared by the blacksmiths in the VAF mess that convinced me a

New Era had arrived. With practically no effort I became acclimated to this newer, nicer war.

So acclimated in fact that, reaching Hollandia, three hours to the west in Dutch New Guinea and meeting one of the guys, I beat him to the punch, asking, "Ya' got any cold beer?" A year earlier that question would probably have gotten me a coarse laugh and a padded cell; in Hollandia it got me a beer, warm, but still beer. And all I had to do was ask. My aching back!

Yes, our Army, "the damn Yanks," had picked up, left Australia and moved north, lock, stock, barrel. This, at first glance, may not appear too remarkable, but I doubt that the utter complexity and immense proportions of what our Army has had to do and is still doing as it moves northward can possibly be imagined by what we mil'try refer to as the lay mind.

Grabbing a beachhead a task force has on hand a beach, large areas of up-and-down, heavily wooded country, a couple of sunken Jap barges and a number of Jap bodies, a quantity of shell holes and bomb craters, a few tattered grass shacks infested with scrub typhus,

151

and a battered, cratered, non-operational air strip or so covered with a lot of twisted wreckage, once a part of the Japanese air force, on capture of no value whatsoever except as watchbands. Of roads, docks, water, telephone lines, lights, shelter, buildings or food there are none, not one stick, but there are fifty or sixty thousand Yanks or more, all crying for large quantities of everything, including such items as teletypes, beam stations, fluorescent lights, automobile sub-assembly plants, dentist's drills, and electric refrigerators. And because it is composed of Americans, the task force must have its comforts—a PX, movies, fresh bread, salt and pepper, an officer's club. In a matter of weeks it will have them, where once there was nothing.

Well, the following is a partial list of some of the hundreds of signs that flanked the thirty-mile stretch of twisting, dusty road between Sentani Strip and Hollandiatown in September, 1944, when Hollandia was at its height as a base:

Speed 20 MPH	Sentani Strip	PX WHSE
DIV HQ Speed 8 MPH	—— Engineer Const Co WATER POINT	—— Engineer Pipeline Co.
Queen Wilhelmina Highway	DON'T WASTE WATER	NICA HQ SWPA
S CURVE	ESQUIRE THEATRE	4th Platoon —— QM Bakery Co.
THE DUSTBOWL American Red Cross Canteen	—— QM TRUCK CO (Amph)	No Vehicles Beyond This Point
—— Petroleum Distribution Co.	2d Platoon Co B —— Signal Air Warning Battalion	SLOW CURVE
LITTLE YONKERS BALL PARK	NAVAL BASE	PIPELINE 3 Feet

I have often wondered about the hungry little slant-eyes, left to die by the Imperial Japanese Army. Peering down through the rain forest at the Americans. Americans who, apparently oblivious of the presence of several thousand enemies, worked twenty-four hours a day at remodeling the face of old New Guinea, building in a matter of weeks roads, airstrips, campsites resembling the Grand Coulee and a two lane, all-weather highway over hills and through valleys where the present denizens of the rain forest, in two years, had succeeded in grubbing out a single, muddy rutted track; Americans who then pounded that highway to pieces with every known kind of wheeled and tracked vehicle from motorcycles and freight-hoists to twenty-ton portable ditch-diggers; Americans who built and built

and built and hauled and issued until fifty or sixty thousand of them were adequately, even comfortably housed, decently clothed and fed, and well enough generally that they could complain bitterly about a lack of real potatoes or cold beer; Americans who, on D-plus-60 or D-plus-less if all went well, flew Red Cross girls across a thousand miles of jungle to serve coffee in their growing base; Americans who flew nonchalantly overhead day after day in C-47's laden with foodstuffs, all the paraphernalia of war, more Americans, wine even; Americans who sometimes erected motion picture screens then dug foxholes . . . I've often wondered just exactly what the stranded little slant-eyes who were privileged to see us at work thought of old Tanaka and his plan.

As the Army moved north, The Professor had preceded me and moved with it. He left Tville early in the year, boarding with some assistance a C-47 on a cool misty morning after a solid week of farewell parties that wrote an epilogue to the legend that was Townsville. He reached Moresby a little the worse for some weather over the Coral Sea, and established himself there and then. But as we grabbed Hollandia and Moresby folded, he parked his long brown overcoat and muffler (The Professor was never one to throw anything away) and moved again, flying into Hollandia on D-plus-10 or 12 or thereabouts. He arrived, as was usual with The Professor, without baggage of any kind—somehow, somewhere between Jackson and Sentani Strips he lost it.

At Hollandia again there were first rumors of WACs, then anticipation, and finally the WACs themselves. I was more or less prepared to hear—or rather overhear—that, "Forty WACs are coming in tomorrow." I took the news quite calmly, and when The Professor, a week or so later, came plunging into our tent babbling, "The WACs are here!" I said quietly, "Yes? Where?" And lunged through our screen door, a pair of field glasses pressed close to my chest. The property of the Far East Air Force (trust the Air Corps to get in on the ground floor of a good thing) the forty WACs went into a prepared camp about a quarter of a mile away, on the far side of several thicknesses of barbed wire and under the watchful eye of what appeared to be nearly a company of MPs, all armed to the teeth. More FEAF WACs followed the original forty, then came FFE WACs (property of United States Army Forces in the Far East) GHQ WACs, USASOS WACs until eventually Hollandia was so full of WACs that a man could scarcely leave his tent without his pants on.

Now a number of soldiers, ourselves included, knowing darn well that some of us would be forced to "wait on them," had about decided that their presence would warrant more trouble than they would be worth. WACs on the spot, however, our manly utterances went by the board, like that, and we joined, enthusiastically the daily stampede that rolled toward the WAC detachment.

Considering the rigmarole that was a necessary part of dating a WAC, we sometimes wondered, even after their arrival, if the results were worth the effort, but continued to stampede. Actually dating *a* WAC, or at least *a* FEAF WAC, was impossible. The dear things were allowed beyond their enclosure—colloquially known as Dachau—only in twos or multiples thereof, a system that certainly put the damper on a lot of enthusiastic GI planning. Found alone with a WAC, one—and likewise the WAC—was subject to some kind of disciplinary action. Assuming that we knew a WAC and were willing to include a few of her friends in our plans, and could reach her by phone—a feat in itself, since LIGHTNING 149, was busy from around, I would guess, 0530 until 2400 hours each day and busier than that on week-ends—we had then to persuade our WAC that on the evening in question we could surpass in kinds and quantities of dainties (tomato juice, olives, cold beer, a radio, etc.) any other offers that she may have had. May have had, hell! Always had. We loathed this state of affairs with all our hearts, but the WACs had a good thing and they knew it and some of them drove a hard bargain in spite of our screams: "Girlie, this war won't last forever!" Our cajoling successful, our WAC would agree to round up some other WACs—we might state a preference but there was no guarantee that

anything would come of it—and "put our name on the book." Then, at 1700 or 1430 on some days, we would drive over to the encampment, park our jeep about two hundred yards this side of the MP control point, necessarily walk the rest of the way (because, we surmised, a walking man is a better target) and present ourselves at the MP post guarding the WAC dayroom. Had our WAC remembered to put our names on the book and did the MP succeed in finding and deciphering them, and if we were in a proper uniform (shorts, as I learned one day to my embarrassment, were not acceptable) we were allowed inside, through a kind of barbed-wire-and-burlap chute faintly reminiscent of the entrance to a flight trap. Once inside, we waited—and waited and waited and waited just as in civilian days—for our dates. The dayroom was watched over and order therein assured by two more MPs, armed and twirling nightsticks, who generally looked as if they wished they were someplace else. Its atmosphere, in all, I have seen surpassed in gaiety by a number of city morgues.

Since most of the FEAF WACs we knew worked at rather irregular hours, chiefly as telephone operators, secretaries, typists, file clerks or communications girls, collecting the five or six we'd bargained for at odd moments during the evening and in the face of the no-lone-WACs rule entailed operating an involved shuttle service that would, I think, have given an experienced troop movements man a few bad moments. Briefly, two would get us one. But those two and the one they got us had each to be accompanied by an armed escort, which made a total of six or one more than Base had authorized in a jeep. Consequently one of us armed escorts always scrunched down and made a noise like a jack handle while passing the MP control points. Or on occasion, though it was a little risky, if short a WAC, one of us pulled a fatigue hat low over his ears and rode through the control point necking, brazenly, with another of us—and making a noise like a WAC.

Faced with the problem of returning and checking in a large and uneven number of WACs before 2345 hours and with several of us perhaps, in an alcoholic state that automatically barred our getting within five hundred yards of the encampment, we were forced to get our shuttle service underway again a full hour in advance of the deadline. Following a couple of our more hilarious evenings I have

returned as many as three separate and distinct WACs, at twenty-minute intervals, to the ill-disguised admiration of the MPs, who probably thought of me as a kind of poor man's Bluebeard.

In Hollandia proper (Hollandiatown) life was a little better. The USASOS WACs, sitting high up in the chain of supply located near the docks and within easy reach of two battalions of Sea Bees, were in a position to promote things that would improve their lot, and our lot with them. Besides, they were evidently, in the vernacular, "a bunch of operators," and operate they did, building a large Rec Hall complete with booths, dance floor, orchestra pit and bar, mostly of plywood euphemistically referred to as "scrap lumber." They held dances two or three times a week that were probably the ultra of Hollandia's social whirl. Hard-won bottles of one thing or another might be taken to these affairs. There was even, on some nights, a stag line of—my aching back!—WACs! The USASOS WACs were proud of their roadhouse and rightly so. To begin with they'd nothing but an area, too full of rocks and holes to be of much use, plus the idea. On the pretext of leveling a volleyball court they'd gotten some Sea Bees who hadn't seen a white woman in fourteen months to come over on their afternoon off, with a bulldozer, and scrape the area. Some of the Sea Bees agreed to come back the following day and through the efforts of a couple of the prettier and cleverest WACs were prevailed upon to leave their bulldozer overnight, parked behind the messhall. That night the WACs "took their names off the book," and thus, with the help of the innocent MPs assigned to the detachment entrance, effectively prevented the Sea Bees from reclaiming their bulldozer. In a like manner they acquired other tools, and other Sea Bees and once or twice some simple-minded Army engineers, enticed over for an afternoon, built the Rec Hall a little at a time. They kept their laborers in material through various other nefarious methods, chicanery and out and out vamping among them, and for a time mention of a 6x6-foot sheet of plywood or a keg of 6-penny nails was the quickest way to a USASOS WAC's heart. The hall completed, they invited the original Sea Bees to the opening night and returned the hot dozer, which was, after all, a nice gesture. On paper, of course, their establishment didn't exist. I got the above from a bright-eyed little staff sergeant who admitted, practically hugging herself with glee, that stealing their Rec Hall, with their own little hands, had been a lot of fun. She admitted too, that her tent mates could probably acquire a Quonsett hut and the services of some Sea Bees who would make of it a swimming pool, if only the girls would put their minds to it. She would rather, she said, have in the vicinity a nice friendly battalion of Sea Bees than all the Red Cross, U.S.O., and Special Service companies or officers then overseas . . .

The WACs, I guess, though we even referred to them as "dehydrated sex," were mighty nice to have around.

CHOO CHEE

THE PROFESSOR was a kind of poor man's Trader Horn.

A still-growing legend of The Professor's rise from his rags to relative riches in a little under two months may one day make a brilliant commentary on the abacadabra of requisitioning through channels. Hollandia at the time, but recently wrested from the Japanese, was a growing base. More troops than supplies, as is apparently always the case, were pouring in via sea and air. The supply situation generally was in the usual chaos: nobody knew where anything or anybody else was located. Half a dozen higher headquarters were knocking everybody's priorities on matériel, labor and cargo space into a cocked hat. Nobody had enough of anything; if they were commissioned they sent people after some saying only, "Get it, I don't care how."

The Professor made his first deal with a captain desperately in need of light sockets who doubted that the two men he'd sent out to steal some would get enough. He gave The Professor a pair of pliers. How or through what channels The Professor came into some light sockets I don't know, but come into them he

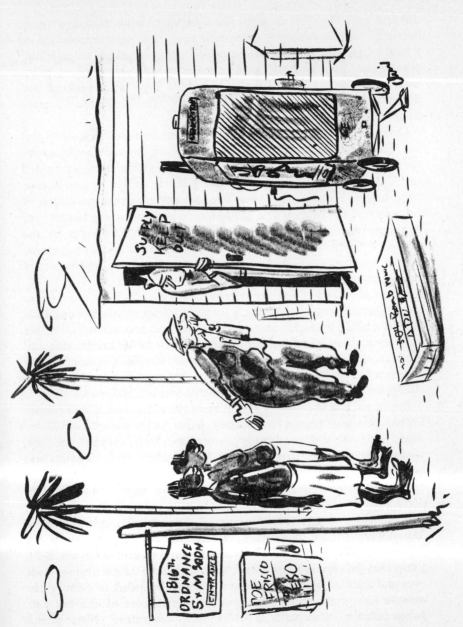

did and gave them to the captain, thus acquiring a friend, a "connection," and in return a pyramidal tent. His tent established as a kind of base of operations, he sallied forth in search of anything else he could use and any troop carrier group, personnel or pilots with whom he could do business. He found the latter without any difficulty to speak of and bequeathed them certain valuable "connections" that he'd kept alive in Tville.

On their next trip south the troop carriers brought back some gin, and The Professor's split, less a certain amount for social obligations, became almost a kind of legal tender. Not that he brazenly traded any Colonel some gin for a jeep but a bottle of gin or promise of same, held in abeyance, has been known to crumble the resolution of a number of the officers and gentlemen who control the issuance of all things from stationery to plumbing. The Professor's gin, by the time he'd acquired a jeep, a floor and a framework and some screening for his tent, some plywood, a phone and a dozen odd uniforms and accessories, was pretty well depleted.

When another Fat Cat flight replenished his stock he went on to bigger, better things, acquiring a discarded drop chute that as a kind of false ceiling made his tent much cooler and aroused considerable envy on the part of infrequent female visitors, an ice connection and often enough meal privileges with a near-by battalion of Sea Bees, an overhaul job on his jeep, electric lights. He even had his hooks into a sergeant in a medical supply depot that stocked iceboxes.

But of all The Professor's acquisitions the most unique was a small brown Javanese manservant named Julius, who shined our shoes, made our beds, did our laundry, swept the floor, cleaned the tent, washed our messkits, carried water, hauled away empty bottles and beer cans, and aroused the envy of all our visitors. A native of Samarang, Java, Julius, sixteen, the oldest of eight, had been deported by the Japanese to Halmaheira as a colonel's Number One boy and gone along with the colonel, scarcely through choice, to Manokwari, thence Noemfoor, where, on our landing there we Americans—liberated him. He was evacuated to Hollandia via B-24, a trip that Julius was wont to recount with little or no urging, wide eyes and a lot of wildly impressive gestures intended to convey the massive size, great speed and four roaring motors of the big Lib. Julius called it, incidentally, a "B-24" or a "Liberator." None of this great brown bird stuff for him.

CHOO CHEE
CHOO CHEE

Once in Hollandia, Julius became the nominal property and ward of Netherlands East Indies Civil Administration. Already acquainted with the NICA authorities, The Professor noted with his rheumy little eyes that NICA had no electric lights and he made them a proposition; for three boys he would get them electric lights. The enterprising Dutch had snapped at the offer and promptly produced three boys; The Professor had just as promptly traded two of them (to a first lieutenant of ordnance) for a generator, wiring, sockets, bulbs and a detail to install them. NICA was satisfied—they had plenty of boys. The lieutenant was satisfied—he had plenty of generators. And The Professor retained as his brokerage the odd boy.

On joining The Professor Julius spoke Javanese, Malayan, passable Dutch and a smattering of Japanese. He soon acquired a fair command of Americanese—considerably faster, at least, than we with all our little English-Malayan dictionaries ever acquired more than a nodding acquaintance with Malayan. We did learn *choo chee choo chee* meaning wash, to wash, washing or laundry; *bagoose* meaning good, okay; *tetabagoose* meaning bad, no good, a synonym almost, for Japanese; and *gela gela* meaning crazy, off your head, or under the particular circumstances in which Julius used with it, with gestures, drunk. But we were thankful for Julius' linguistic abilities. The first three words that he learned from us, incidentally, with an accuracy, were: "gin," "jeep" and "goddamn." No simple brown man exactly Julius had been, in Samarang, a motion picture (or *biascope*) fanatic. Thanks to the Overseas Motion Picture Service he could in Hollandia resume his first nighting; and he did, disappearing at 1700 sharp each day, aimed in the general direction of the nearest camp movie, or "GI show." He saw, I think, all the current hits within a radius of twelve miles of Sentani Strip. His heroes, no latter day Klieg lights, were Charlie Chaplin, Ken Maynard, Rin Tin Tin and Errol Flynn.

Julius had other accomplishments. He could and often did sing for us or for his own amusement—"The Beer Barrel Polka" in Javanese (which was something, believe me); the Javanese national anthem in Dutch; Javanese love songs in his own inimitable fashion which all but brought swaying palms, moonlight lagoons and undulating Balinese into our very tent; and "Mairzy Doates" in English. A quaint and strangely exotic sight was Julius, our faithful little brown manservant, pattering up from the creek, with a flower in his hair and his shanks in a pair of GI shorts, his arms full of laundry, to the lilting notes of "Mairzy Doates and dozey doates and little lambsy divey . . ." if that be English. We tried to teach him "Shoo Shoo Baby" but were stymied by Julius' trouble with "H's," a vocal booby trap that resulted in his gurgling "Soo Soo Babee," then going off into gales of laughter. *Soo soo*, we eventually learned one day when Julius got his hands on a pin-up, meant, in Javanese, milk, and to Julius that for which Balinese dancing girls are supposedly noted.

To begin with Julius had but one fault—his preoccupation with the *choo chee choo chee*. Unless plainly ordered not to, he *choo chee choo chee*'d every day, singing "Mairzy Doates" the while,

166

every scrap of clothing that we were careless enough to leave lying around. Whether it was dirty or not made little difference to Julius, and on too many occasions, changing our pants, we would find the reasonably fresh pair we'd been saving gone. Questioned, Julius would declare that they were *choo chee choo chee*. Resigned to the dirtier pair, we often found that they, in the meantime, had also become *choo chee* and had disappeared, sometimes forever, since unless we were on the premises when the *choo chee* came back and was divided somebody else invariably claimed them. Or if nobody claimed them Julius grabbed them, marked them, for reasons best known to himself, "Toan P 73" and stuck them in The Professor's barracks bag.

Aside from this overt zeal with the *choo chee* Julius was at first a perfect servant, but—as a Mr. Berger of NICA had warned us would happen—we spoiled him, and Julius, presently, was well nigh worthless. So worthless, in fact, that NICA and Mr. Berger refused to accept him as a trade-in on a good boy. So we were stuck with Julius, who daily grew more lax in his duties, disappeared for hours at a time, ignored empty water cans, took in *choo chee* on the side and *choo chee*'d it on our time to his profit, and with his by then all too excellent command of English saying with great persuasiveness and expressive gestures, when sent off to expedite some task he didn't particularly relish, "Me no understand." In the end, as had our Australian compatriots before, Julius got on to the "holidays" racket. Professing Christianity, he took Sundays off, also any Holy Days that turned up, and if he learned of them in time our own holidays—Labor Day, Columbus Day, Armistice Day and so on. Now and then, absent for a day, he would explain with utter simplicity when questioned next morning, that it had been a Mohammedan religious feast ... We are wondering what will happen to Julius come Yom Kippur. And have decided that we are not, in any measure, the colonists the Dutch are.

THE PHILIPPINES. For two years we had been saying, "That'll be the day!" It wasn't the historical significance. Our battle cry was, "When are we going home?"

Between us and the Golden Gate stood the PIs, and we gathered that we'd see there three things that we were starving to see again—roads, houses and people.

Now The Day was at hand. In Ops shacks and on C-47's, in the lines winding toward Red Cross canteens, in mess halls and in latrines (especially the latter), in pyramidal tents and GI trucks and officers' clubs, on barges and on beaches, on freight docks and in the shade of B-24's, in warehouses, casual camps, everywhere—except possibly, among the CIC (Counter Intelligence Corps) a notoriously clam-headed clan—there was not very guarded talk: When? Where? How soon d'ya think? Manila? That'll be the day . . .

It was time to sink New Guinea below another horizon. Assigned to the 24th Infantry Division I left Wilkins Beach (and New Guinea!) late one afternoon in a Navy LCM with perhaps a dozen other soldiers of one category or another, likewise leaving the Island

—they sincerely hoped—once and for all. Our M boiled out across the harbor in search of Attack Transport 41, a converted Liberty loaded to the smokestack with the bulk of the battalion I was tagging, past the hundreds of ships of all the species in the invasion aquarium that filled Hollandia's harbor until, looking down on them from the heights above Pim's Jetty, it almost seemed that people might walk across the harbor on their decks.

A lone bright star hung high in the west, winking, winking, like a Fitzpatrick travelogue . . . "Aloha, Aloha to old New Guinea . . ." Somebody answered, from the heart, "Well, I hope-t'-christ I never see the goddamn Island again!"

Our APA, as I have mentioned, was—as usual—loaded to the smokestack. It was said that a number of junior officers were quartered in the smokestack. I don't know about that, but I have come to the conclusion, after maybe two and a half months aboard troopships, that there will *never* be enough ships. Not at least, in our theater, where ships have always been worth their weight in cold beer and overloaded on every trip that I've experienced.

Our particular APA was the flagship of a transport division, and in accordance with quaint old navy tradition hung with signs, on everything above the weather decks, "Officers' Country—Enlisted Ranks KEEP CLEAR," and, so a first lieutenant told me, on the bridge deck and up, "Admirals' Country—All Other Ranks KEEP CLEAR." That left us enlisted personnel the weather decks, exclusive of that space taken up by gun mounts, winches, hatch covers, cradled Higgins boats and a deckload of jeeps, 37-mm. guns, weapons carriers and quarter-ton trailers. The broad reaches of sweeping white deck that I've seen mentioned in stories of the sea are apparently a pulp writer's dream; on all the ships I've seen there's been no sweep of deck extending more than eight feet in any direction and those eight feet were steel, studded with rivet heads and covered with a thin layer of rust, oil and cigarette butts.

Still, these decks make a fair bed, if a man can sleep comfortably curled over a cleat. I shared a cozy little nook with a soldier from Tennessee and slept rolled in a poncho under an ambulance whose red crosses on a field of white had been covered with great splotches of green paint. My partner grew a little punchy on about the third night from rising up and banging his head on the transmission, but it

169

could have been worse. At least the oil pan didn't leak as had the oil pan on a truck I'd slept under once. Our nook, in fact, was so cozy that on the night it rained we didn't wake up until the water backed up against the hatch to a depth of about two inches. We woke up then all right, with a fair share of the night's precipitation inside our ponchos, crawled out and stumbled aft, where a kindly guard let us stand under a warm air vent until dawn.

Eventually I became acquainted with the battalion sergeant-major, an earnest young man slowly cracking under the strain of fitting one hundred nine men into one hundred beds, and through him acquired a sack of my own, the lowest in a tier of the usual four. It was situated in a dark after corner of troop compartment 104-A, an extremely desirable location really, since the ventilator next it—in spite of a warning sign: BREAKING HOLES IN THE VENTILATOR SHAFT WILL NOT MAKE THE COMPARTMENT COOLER—had several sizeable holes in its shaft, through which a cool stream of air played over the naked bodies of those who slept in the immediate vicinity. There was a soldier upstairs in our tier who slept (fitfully) with his shoes on, and each night I collected a fair share of the trash his shoes had collected during the course of the day.

Late in the afternoon of the fourth day the speaker system announced nasally that all troops . . . all troops would lay below to their compartments . . . lay below to their compartments, and that division officers would make their readiness for sailing reports . . . readiness for sailing reports. . . . All the troops did not lay below to their compartments, but enough card games were broken up and sleeping soldiers awakened and driven to their feet so that the petty officer of the anchor watch, by yelling stand-clear-there-and-you-men-move-aft and so on pretty regularly and in emergencies pushing a little, cleared enough winches and deck of soldiers that his watch might raise the anchor. On all sides of us other ships, soldiers and anchor watches were apparently going through the same routine, and as our three long columns of landing craft, landing ships and transports, flanked by honest-to-God shooting navy, stood out to the open sea Hollandia's harbor seemed, suddenly, empty of ships. Our convoy headed north; and at sundown, as the speaker system intoned "Division Officers make your readiness to darken ship reports . . . readiness to darken ship reports," New Guinea was but a darker purple blur on the southern edge of the world. And then it was gone, with no regrets.

Like landings, all convoys are alike, differing only in details of misery. Our Leyte convoy was no exception. There were roughly 1400 troops aboard our APA and at any given moment of the day or night I could, without any effort to speak of, touch at least eight of the other 1399.

As our convoy crawled northward under a blistering sun we bowed to the ship's speaker system and the fact that no matter where we should have liked to sit, upwards of five hundred other soldiers had already had the same idea. In a theater where, it seems, half the navy is ashore and half the army is afloat we dogies have learned to say "fore" and "aft," "port" and "starboard," "stand clear" and "go below" as well as the next man. (The next man happens to be a deep water sailor from the Ozarks with six weeks of Great Lakes Naval behind him.)

APA 41's speaker system was of a particularly strident, monotonous character. It announced "General Quarters, General Quarters, Man your battle stations, Man your battle stations" at dawn and dusk each day with just the same degree of cold mechanical detachment that it used in announcing, on one occasion, "Private first class Hooleybell, William L., U.S. Army, lay aft to the quarter deck and get your dog tags." It announced boat drills, sick call, changes of the watch, "chow—crew only; chow—crew only," "chow—troops only; chow—troops only," "sweepers, man your brooms, clean and sweepdown fore 'n aft." Once it announced that anyone wishing to part with a pint of blood should lay aft to the sick bay—a suggestion that drew little response that I could see, the general attitude being that in all likelihood we might well need that pint of blood ourselves. On another occasion, intoning the news, the system informed us that 20,000 bobby socks of various ages had stormed the Paramount to see Sinatra. We responded to that all right. As a matter of fact a quorum in troop compartment 104-A devoted nearly an hour to Sinatra. One soldier brought forth, whether truthfully or not I can't say, that some studio recently spent $5000 to have Frankie's teeth straightened; a second soldier from that point on devoted his share of the discussion to muttering, over and over, "I'll straighten his teeth."

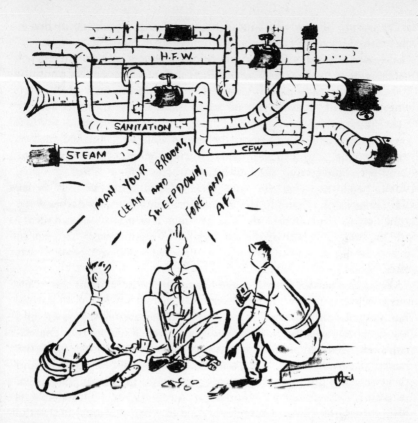

Once a day we had boat drill. All troops would lay below to their compartments, untangle and struggle into their equipment and as directed by the speaker system ("First wave—move out; first wave move out") stumble up the companionways to their respective boat stations. These drills were a little confused the first few days and often enough a hundred or more soldiers would line up with their eyes on the same LCVP (capacity 36). About three days out some big wheel had another bright idea, and a cargo net was forthwith rigged over the front of the bridge. If we were caught we practiced ascending and descending this net a couple of times a day. Otherwise we sat or lay or sprawled in what shade we could find, reading, smoking, talking, playing endless games of cards or simply staring off into space, wishing we were some place else.

When about five days out we were briefed. Squatting in the sun on Number Four Hatch we listened to an earnest, inarticulate first lieutenant outline where we would land, when, in what order, with what to back us up and in the face of what probable opposition. The lieutenant was a little vague about the details and stuck on the horns of an old briefing dilemma—to prepare us for the worst (the fact that some of us would be killed) without lessening in any way our confidence in the eventual success of the operation. He need not have worried, I guess; we were chiefly concerned with getting it over with and getting the hell in out of the sun.

We began to count the days—not as days left to live, but as days left aboard ship. Possibly the dirt and heat and sweat aboard a troop-ship have a kind of payoff. I know that I was *looking forward* to the landing, and most of the soldiers felt the same way. We wanted above all else to get the hell off the boat—we'd take our chances after that.

At supper on D-minus-1 we ate standing (of course) in the troops' mess, elbow to elbow, while somebody with a bucketful of hot coffee barged around behind us. On deck afterwards there was a lot of the usual talk about what we would each eat if we could. That talk subsided presently and the weather decks were more quiet than usual. It was that hour between the dark and the daylight, the last peaceful, tranquil hour that most of us would know for some weeks to come, that some of us would ever know. By tacit consent we left each other alone and, leaning over a lifeline or on a jeep or a winch, thought our own thoughts. We talked again after Taps, in troop compartment 104-A. Rather subdued talk, it was, but it seemed somehow a little silly to sleep that last night. Some slept, of course, and snored, and some told dirty jokes.

General Quarters was piped at dawn and we troops lay below to our compartments. A few of the bolder spirits promptly slipped topside again to see what was going on and I joined them, not because I am a bolder spirit but because of my nervous system. There wasn't much of anything happening. To the north, west and south of us, barely visible on the horizon, was a lot of low, blue murky land—the Philippines.

Behind and on both sides of us the rest of the convoy spread away in diminishing sizes to the horizon; some miles ahead of us battlewagons were shelling the beach. At intervals great, ragged, dirty blobs of brown smoke and vicious, stabbing fists of yellow flame belched in the sky beyond their turrets; seconds later the dull, crunching *whump* of the broadside would reach us. Now and then somebody with a pair of field glasses, watching a brace of palm trees lift bodily into the air, yelped, "Geezuzz! Did ya' see that!"

I don't remember quite how it started now, but suddenly, all around us, people were breathing, "Air raid!" The desire to see was stronger than the desire to duck—half a dozen of us scrambled atop a cradled LCVP. Far away to the southwest—I heaved a mental sigh of relief at just how far away—black splotches of flak were filling the sky. More bursts appeared, then more, leading eastward. Half a dozen people yelled, "There goes! See him! Sonavabitch!"

A fading, ragged, still lengthening trail of flak hung high up across the southern sky, and astern of us by now a lone plane (a Betty, somebody guessed) circled lazily over the convoy. A fresh handful of flak popped black in the sky around it. We cheered lustily. The Betty went into a shallow dive. More flak splattered black against the sky behind it. We screamed and fell over each other and gun mounts and stanchions, scrambling for a better look. The Betty levelled off and disappeared to the northwest. Like the passing of a sudden thunderstorm, our air raid was over. "Geezuzz!" we told each other, "Did ya' see that!" We were referring to the apparent inaccuracy of our anti-aircraft.

The battlewagons were closer now, the *whump* of their broadsides something to wait for and wince under. A heavy gray pall of smoke hung low over the coastline. Gray divebombers, like roustabouts pounding a tent stake, peeled off one after another, dropped straight down on Hill 552—a knobby customer commanding the beach—pulled out. Gray blobs of dust and smoke blossomed behind them.

At 0730 we were peremptorily ordered back to our compartments, and from the cursing and shouting and bumping and banging and squealing of winches over our heads gathered that the boats were being lowered. At about 0800 the speaker system moaned: "First wave—stand by; first wave—stand by." There may have been a time, once, when people, at this point, ground out between clenched teeth, "This is it!" That phrase, now, induces vomiting. The fighting words I overheard were: "Gimme alight, fella," and "Well, here we go again."

The first wave moved out presently, the second wave stood by for fifteen or twenty minutes then followed them topside. A few minutes later our wave, the third, stumbled up the companionways. Our boat, an LCM, was waiting, banging nastily against the side of the ship under the after port cargo net. Three at a time we turned our backsides into the wind, went over the side and swung clumsily down the net. A couple of soldiers lost their helmets in the struggle. A medium tank, complete with crew, filled most of our M. Some thirty of us passengers arranged ourselves around it, took off our helmets, lit cigarettes. Our M swung away and joined five other Ms circling aimlessly a few hundred yards off the stern of our APA. All around us other tight little circles of VPs and Ms were going round and round in the water near their respective APAs. They looked, somehow, like well-disciplined broods of ducklings, and their APAs, it follows naturally, like fat, placid, watchful mother ducks.

Somebody, seeing a line of Alligators (amtracks, lightly armed and armored) and Buffaloes (amtracks, more heavily armed and armored) churning through the water some distance way, yelled, "There goes the first wave!" There was a momentary quickening of interest in our M, that subsided as the first wave, drawing away, became so many churning, white frothy wakes topped with antennae. We didn't talk much. What conversation there was was mostly about other landings we had seen and the possibilities of this one. I wasn't thinking about anything in particular.

At about 0900 we broke our circle and headed shoreward in a ragged V formation. Again there was a momentary quickening of interest that again subsided as we throttled down. The sun was softening the tar that waterproofed our tank. I sneaked a couple of swallows out of one of my canteens.

The third wave off our APA, our M, together with other Ms from other APAs, actually formed the fifth assault wave, due on the beach at H-plus-20. As we neared the shore the ends of our V swung out and forward, and for the first time we looked like a wave.

There was a general adjusting of helmets. Somebody yelled, "Mortars!" Ahead and to our left two foamy white geysers of water rose straight up out of the deep blue of the bay. There was a general movement toward the ramp deck of our M. We were close in now, things whirred and whizzed through the air somewhere above our heads, we heard the sharp, distinctive "pop!" of Japanese rifle fire . . . The movement accelerated; some of us squirmed in behind the tank; others cringed against its sides. I flattened on the after deck of the M. One of the crew yelled that it would be a wet landing. We throttled down and with a slight jar, grounded.

There was a momentary whirring of steel cables, the ramp of our LCM went down with a thumping splash. We lurched forward in a kind of melee, hesitated an instant, one by one, at the edge of the ramp, dropped off into waist deep surf, and sprinted—insofar as anybody can sprint over shifting sand in water to his waist with forty varied pounds of equipment dragging him down—the twenty odd yards to the beach. The whizzing and buzzing and popping that I have mentioned was suddenly much louder. Terribly loud, as a matter of fact.

This was combat. There was no excitement. Instead there was fear. Plenty of it. I remember that on my first landing I was scared blue twenty-four hours a day for fourteen days. Through successive landings my fear was less continuous. I learned to distinguish between our mortars and their mortars; our machine guns and theirs;

our rifle shots and the sharp pop of a Jap 25. I learned to quit leaping and trembling when I heard our own 105s and 155s. Landing on Leyte, I was delighted to find that for several hours at a time I was hardly scared at all.

But not at night. We Americans do our best dirty work in the daytime; the Japs do theirs at night. Between 10 P.M. and daylight I have conjured up as many as eight *banzai* charges. And I have prayed on those nights, almost steadily for but one thing—dawn. On a couple of such occasions—both on Leyte—there was some frantic firing in the immediate vicinity and dawn, on both occasions, disclosed dead Japanese, also in the immediate vicinity.

And it is at night, of course, that we are bombed. Sporadically, ineffectively, with slight damage and casualties, the communiques say. But there is nothing sporadic or ineffective about the way you crouch, praying in a hole. Praying feverishly that you are not one of the casualties. I look back at raids that were hardly nuisance attacks, but the bombs that whistled down upon us sent me crouching in a hole doing my level best to crawl inside my helmet with the almost certain knowledge that my posterior—which wouldn't fit into any helmet under any circumstances—presented itself to the sky as a huge, glowing bulls-eye.

There was an Australian correspondent with us on Gloucester, a scrawny little man who had survived the London blitz in its entirety. While the rest of us would lie groveling in a half-demolished, log-covered Jap dugout, he would sit topside listening intently and entertaining us with a running account of the Jap's activities. "The ba-a-a-stard," he would say. "He's circling now, out over the shipping." (We would relax a little.) "No, he's coming back." (We would try to crawl further inside our helmets.) "Theah. The ba-a-a-stard's diving. Hear him?" (We heard him all too plainly.) "There goes his bloody bomb. Hear 'er click?" I did eventually learn to wait for and catch the barely audible click as the bomb left the rack—an utterly useless accomplishment. One time he did not guess the bomb's fall, but came tumbling himself into the hole on top of us. A great roaring, tearing rush of air seemed to follow him, and then a blast that seemed to shatter the world.

I have yet to approach by several hundred raids anything like his *sang-froid*.

The next worse thing is rain. The utter misery that such a simple thing as rain can make out of a man's life is hard to imagine. Oh, I'd been caught in a shower now and then and come home under the impression that I was "soaked." Hell, as a civilian I rather liked a rainy day now and then. On Cape Gloucester—where I won my letter, so to speak—there were eleven consecutive rainy days. We got wet and stayed wet eleven consecutive days. There isn't a single solitary thing that I can think of that is not adversely affected by rain: matches, cigarettes, cigarette lighters, guns, cameras, film, cof-

fee, adhesive tape, leggings, underwear, socks, shoes, K-ration, C-ration, chocolate bars, razor blades, toothpaste, eating, sleeping, walking, sitting. . . . Try it once. Try *anything*, standing under a shower.

Yes, I hate rain. I hate rain and I hate bombs and I hate nights and I hate fear. Somewhere along the line I learned to hate Japs. At first when I came overseas I did not particularly hate the Japanese. I seldom thought about them. I knew no Japanese; they'd none of them done anything to me. I found it much easier to hate a number of our own NCOs. Well, that's all changed. I've crouched and quivered in too many wet holes, while bombs moaned somewhere in the darkness above. I've been soaking wet too many times. I've spent too many sleepless, fear-filled nights.

We've all spent too many fear-filled nights. Anybody who has been through this war down here in these Godforsaken places feels this way. Or, I suppose, through the war anywhere. And especially the infantry; nothing that any government can ever do will begin to repay these men.

The added combat pay they receive is much like offering the carnival employee who dodges baseballs an extra sawbuck to do the same thing in a shooting gallery.